MW01623412

Autism, Art and Art Therapy

A guide for parents

Mia Takada Dill

Copyright © 2016 Mia Takada Dill
All rights reserved

Cover Design by Kenji Takada Dill

Cover Font – Moonlight Serenade; David Kerkhoff

ISBN-10: 099769260X
ISBN-13: 978-0997692600 (Mineko Takada-Dill)

To the families of
people touched by autism

Contents

Mia Takada-Dill

Acknowledgements

My heartfelt appreciation goes out to my family and friends who have accompanied me on this writing path for some time.

I want to thank my husband, Tim Dill, whose love, support and patience deeply nourishes me. Thank you for our talented son, Kenji Takada Dill for the book cover and the Spectrum illustrations.

My special thanks to Hsuan Hua Chang, my business coach who encouraged me to write about Art Therapy and Autism after I completed the certification course on Autism at The University of Washington. The process of creating a book was not easy but at the end I could say it was therapeutic, as is any endeavor of creating art.

My appreciation to Larry Spangler, a licensed occupational therapist and qi-gong practitioner, for his friendship and useful feedback on the manuscript.

Many thanks to my editor and friend, Laurel Turling. Editing a book written by somebody who has never written a book and who is writing in English as a second language was not easy. I recognize your hard work, seeing the book before and after editing.

Mia Takada-Dill

Introduction

My journey to help people through art started when I was a little girl. I was an extremely shy girl and often played alone at recess. Although I did not do well academically, I was good at painting. Painting helped me feel good and praise for my pictures eventually helped me to be an average student at school.

I did not truly feel as though I belonged anywhere until I entered Art College in Tokyo, where I met *unique* people just like me. Over 30 years later, we are still friends and we all work in visual art. Some of us are well known designers and others are art teachers. I chose to be an art therapist after working with children with developmental differences.

Over 25 years ago, I worked as a teacher at a special school in Japan. All of the students had physical difficulties and intellectual disabilities (very low IQ). We mostly worked on life skills, physical therapy, sensory integration therapy, gardening, music and art. While the students needed to be helped to change clothing, feeding and life skills, they were very happy to gain some autonomy when they created art. Some of them had autism, but all of them were called, "mentally retarded" at that time.

Even when I went graduate school at NYU in the early 1990's, we did not talk much about autism in the child development class. When the Diagnostic and Statistical Manual of Mental Disorders (DSM) was published in its 4th edition in 1994, autism was listed as a spectrum disorder including Autistic Disorders, Asperger's Syndrome and PDD-NOS, under the umbrella of Pervasive Developmental Disorders. I was working at the Early Childhood

Program at a Community Mental Health Center in Seattle at that time. I was a teacher/therapist in the early childhood day treatment center, where we began receiving children with PDD-NOS diagnosis and sensory integration problems. Honestly we had no clue what to expect and how they were different from the other children with behavior problems.

In 1998 we had a wonderful opportunity to be educated by University of Washington (UW), Experimental Education Unit (EEU). We observed EEU classrooms and were taught by their outreach staff. The EEU also ran a support group for Asperger's.

Between 2000 and 2010, I worked at Early Childhood Behavior classrooms in various school districts as a Mental Health Counselor. All the children had IEP and behavior difficulties. A part of my job was to understand where those behaviors came from. Some children came from chaotic homes and acted out while others had ADHD, Learning Disabilities and some form of autism. All of them liked visual schedules and a reward system. I worked on ways to engage and support the children's family members. Autism became one of the disability categories under the federal law, the Individuals with Disabilities in Education Act (IDEA) in 2004. We supplied resources so that the families could be assessed for autism but some of them were too scared to be assessed and some were discouraged by their pediatricians. The pediatricians suggested that the parents wait, despite the fact that the doctors themselves did not know what autism was. For the last ten years, most of us who were not educated about autism in our graduate schools struggled to understand it and to help the children to receive the appropriate early treatment.

Between September 2013 and June 2014, I decided to take a certification program on Autism Theory and Practice at University of Washington with Rafael Bernier, PhD, Jim Mancini and other staff at the Children's Autism Clinic, UW Autism Center, and UW Adult Autism Clinic. I also met 16 other classmates who were equally dedicated to help people with Autism Spectrum Disorder (ASD).

The program gave me a basic understanding of autism and the realization that there is very little understanding of autistic art and how to use art as a strength. This is despite many parents of children with ASD acknowledging that their children are skilled in art and enjoy making art. Since the class, I have continued to research and work with many people with Autism and Autism Spectrum Disorder (ASD) in my private practice.

In my practice as an art therapist, I accept each individual diagnosed with autism as a whole person; unique and special. I work with each person one at a time. Some may become leaders in the technology field; others may be working at a grocery store putting groceries in bags. The important part is for all to have full and contented lives regardless of autism and other conditions. I am not sure if autism is curable, but at least you can gain optimal outcome as a result of early diagnosis and appropriate early intervention.

So here I am, ready to share what I know about autism and how we can use art with those touched by autism.

How to use this book

This book is primarily written for parents of children diagnosed with Autism Spectrum Disorder (ASD) who are interested in understanding how to help them develop artistic expression as a strength, recreation, and potentially a career for their future. Simple and comprehensive explorations of autism and treatment options are described as well.

If you decide to have an art therapist in your child's treatment team, make sure you find an art therapist who is knowledgeable regarding ASD. Credentials for art therapists and training are described in Chapter 4.

If you are a treatment provider with a different discipline, such as an ABA therapist, occupational therapist or speech therapist, I would appreciate your feedback. Art could help your clients to open up and be motivated to work on the intense therapy your clients have to go through. At the same time it reflects their symptoms and you need to choose an activity that fits your client's treatment plan.

This book can be used by art therapists without formal training in autism. I love art therapy and would love to have art therapists help people with ASD to have fuller lives.

All art work in this book, except the selections in Chapter 5, was made by me to illustrate the contents. For reasons of privacy, actual art work done by persons with ASD is not included in this book, except for Sam's (not his real name). Sam's mother kindly gifted me his art work when he completed his work with me. I have recreated images similar to those actually made by my clients for illustration.

The illustrations in Chapter 5 are noted with the name of the artist and the origin of the art work. All individuals with ASD portrayed in this book are not actual people, but are fictionalized based on individuals with autism or characteristics of autism.

Vocabulary and abbreviations

Aspie	Term that some adults with Asperger's disorder diagnosis choose to call themselves.
Asperger's Disorder/ Syndrome	Describes autistic people with communication impairment and restricted and repetitive interests without speech impairments. Some people think Asperger's is not in Autism Spectrum Disorder. The diagnosis of Asperger's Disorder was omitted from the diagnostic manual in 2013. Currently people use the term to describe people with above average IQ who struggle in the social and communication arena.
Autistic Spectrum Condition ASC	Term often used by UK researchers instead of Autism Spectrum Disorder. Dr. Baron-Cohen describes this term as less stigmatizing and takes a position that ASC is an extreme of the normal variation of

	autistic traits.
Autism Spectrum Disorder ASD	Term used in current diagnostic manual in the U.S. Describes a group of complex and pervasive neurodevelopmental disorders characterized by impairments in social interactions, interests and activities, and language development.
Autistic individuals (people, teens and children) vs. individuals with Autism (ASD)	There have been long debates about which term is better. Some parents and professionals feel if we say *autistic people*, it defines and discriminates against those people. Some autistic people prefer calling themselves autistic to identify themselves, being proud and taking control. In this book I primarily use *individuals with autism* (ASD). If you find where I have used *autistic people*, it means that for that point, I am taking a different position.
Classic Autism	The term that Oliver Sacks used when he wrote about Temple Grandin in 1994 to differentiate between severely autistic people (nonverbal and withdrawn), and people like Grandin.

Eidetic Memory	The ability to recall images in memory after only brief exposure. Also called photographic memory.
Evidenced-based Practice	Intervention integrating three basic principles: (1) the best available research evidence bearing on whether and why a treatment works, (2) clinical expertise (clinical judgment and experience) to identify each patient's unique health state and diagnosis, their individual risks and benefits of potential interventions, and (3) client preferences and values.
High Functioning Autism	People use this term to talk about people with ASD and low to normal and up to genius IQ levels. As a clinician I like to avoid this term because high functioning sounds like they do not need support. In contrast, they need support on different levels. I use the term *autism with IQ in normal range* instead in my practice but in this book I used this term to describe different needs among a broad range of people.
High Impacted Autism	Classic autism requiring support for daily living. People use this term to

	describe people opposite of high functioning.
ICD International Classification of Disease	The international standard diagnostic tool published by WHO (World Health Organization). Implementation of ICD-10-CM was done in October 2015 for insurance billings.
IDEA Individuals with Disabilities Education Act	A law ensuring services to children with disabilities throughout the nation.
Intellectually Disabled	Describes people with low intelligence quotient.
IQ Intelligence Quotient	Human intelligence as measured by standardized tests such as the Wechsler Intelligence Scale.
Mental Retardation	Historically used to describe people with low IQ. Replaced by the term intellectually disabled.
Neurodevelopmental Disorders	Impairments of the growth and development of the brain or central nervous system, including intellectual disabilities, Autism, Communication Disorders and ADHD/ADD etc.
Neurodiversity	Describes autism as a part of broader sense of a spectrum and

	normal variations of human traits.
Pragmatic Language	Social language skills we use while we interacting with others, such as speaking differently depending on the needs of a listener or situation, taking turns in conversation, understanding others' facial expression and body language, etc.
Reciprocity	In this book it is used to describe social reciprocity, which is mutual response to each other or back-and-forth social interaction
Savant	A person with special advanced specific skills in one area despite having much lower cognitive abilities in others, such as learning disabilities.
TD Typically Developing	Describes people without developmental delays or neurodevelopmental disorder.

Chapter 1

What is Autism?

Understanding autism helps you get appropriate support for your child

Autism is a neurodevelopmental disorder characterized by impairment in social communication skills, and repetitive and/or restricted behaviors. Neurodevelopmental disorders are impairments of the growth and development of the brain or central nervous system. Autism is considered a spectrum disorder, meaning a disorder that includes a range of linked condition.

It is not easy to comprehend what autism is and how specifically it affects each individual. Nonetheless, it is important for you to understand how your child is affected. Understanding the disorder will help you get the support you need for your child and your family. I hope that what you find in this chapter is precise enough to begin to understand Autism and helps you to understand your child.

Autism is a complicated and puzzling condition. For this reason, a puzzle piece logo is widely used for autism support organizations and the logo symbolizes autism all over the world (Figure 1).

Figure 1

The puzzle piece logo was first created in 1963 by the British organization National Autistic Society. On their website, they explain, "The puzzle piece is so effective because it tells us something about autism; our children are afflicted by a puzzling condition; it isolates them from normal human contact and therefore they do not 'fit in'."

Autism Spectrum Disorder-a single term for a range of diverse traits

Leo Kanner and Hans Asperger first identified autism in the early 1940's, and since then autism has been classified in various ways. Kanner published an article, *Autistic Disturbances of Affective Contact* in 1943 on eleven cases of children with "infantile autism". Hans Asperger published the first definition of Asperger's syndrome in 1944. He identified a pattern of behavior and abilities that he called "autistic psychopathy". The pattern included "a lack of empathy, little ability to form friendships, one-sided conversation, intense absorption in a special interest, and clumsy movements." It is commonly said that the paper was based on only four boys. However, Dr. Günter Krämer, of Zürich, who knew Asperger, states that it "was based on investigations of more than 400 children.

Currently, the American Psychiatric Association classifies it as

Autism Spectrum Disorder (ASD).

Even though more is known after 50 years of study, ASD is still puzzling. Indeed, we are still discovering how complex the disorder is. There is debate about whether autism is truly a disorder or simply a set of individual traits. The wide diversity of traits among people with autism is referred to as "neuro-diversity." There are people who are severely impacted by autistic symptoms and who have low apparent IQ. They need to have lifelong support and are unable to care for themselves. On the other hand, a significant population of people in IT and other scientific and technological fields have varied levels of autism and these people are instrumental to the success and growth of these fields. They may not "fit in" socially, but they can offer superior skills in certain fields. Still others may have some autistic tendencies but those tendencies do not interfere with their maneuvering in the world. One could say that people with an ASD **diagnosis** have autistic characteristics which are severe and interfering enough so they need additional therapy and support to live in the world that is not made for them. As the word "spectrum" suggests, people with autism spectrum disorder (ASD) may have challenges that run the ranges of from mild to severe, with different levels of ability and disability. Some may have no functional speech, or may be talkative with a rich vocabulary. He or she may be intellectually disabled or have an average or even genius level of IQ. He may be socially withdrawn or may be socially active, although may struggle understanding social cues and fit in social situations. He may be fixated on lining up toys in a certain order, or have an encyclopedic knowledge of animals or another favorite topic. (Figure 2).

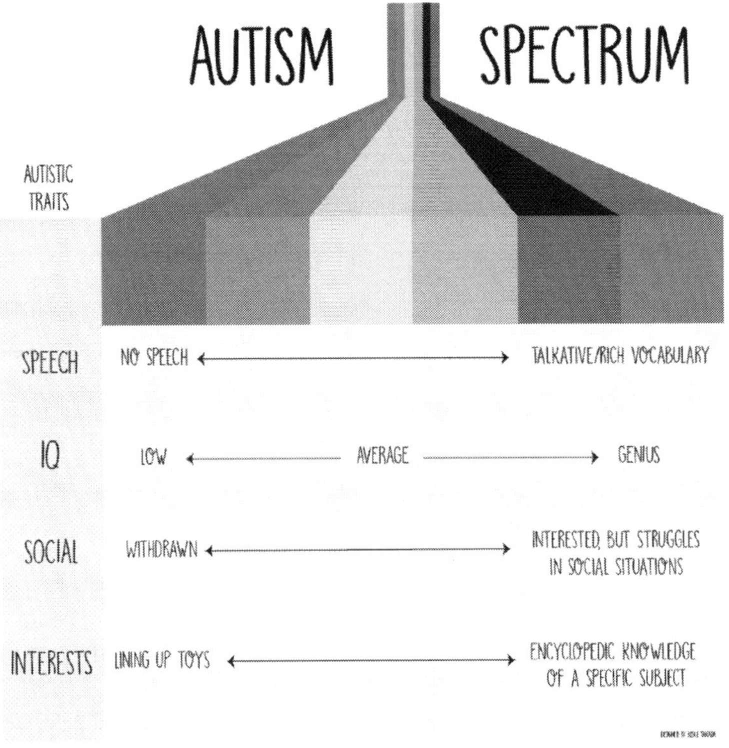

Figure 2.

Please refer to Chapter 2 to read more about diagnosis and intervention.

Autism is called a heterogeneous disorder, meaning that there is a large diversity of symptoms and characteristics. It can be said that every single person who is diagnosed with autism is unique, but all within the common ground of characteristics described below. Furthermore, all of these characteristics are variations to some degree of what is considered typical human development. The term typically developing (TD) refers to people who do not have disabilities severe enough to adversely affect their daily lives. Individuals with ASD are people who need extra assistance to thrive in a world mostly made by and for typically developing people.

In the UK, the term Autistic Spectrum Condition (ASC) is used instead of Autism Spectrum Disorder in order to avoid stigmatizing autism as a disorder. This term also emphasizes the fact that ASC often comes with co-occurring conditions, such as intellectual disabilities or cognitive delays or differences. Many autistic traits are found among the general public and using this term highlights that ASC is an extreme example of the normal variations of autistic traits along the spectrum.

Autism as a development disorder

A basic way to define autism is as a neurodevelopmental disorder with impairment in social communication skills, and repetitive and restricted behaviors. The American Psychiatric Association (APA) publishes the Diagnostic and Statistical Manual of Mental Disorders (DSM), the handbook used by health care professionals as the authoritative guide to the diagnosis of mental disorders. Since the first edition of DSM was published in 1945, autism has had various names. The latest edition, DSM-5, uses the term "Autism Spectrum Disorder." In October 2015, clinicians began using International Classification of Disease (ICD) codes for insurance billing instead of DSM, but it is currently unclear whether ICD codes will impact how the diagnosis is labeled.

How ASD is diagnosed

A diagnosis of ASD is made using behavioral observation-based standardized assessments, in addition to an IQ test. There is no blood test or brain scan to confirm or rule out ASD. In the state of Washington, only trained psychiatrists, neurologists, developmental pediatricians (MDs) and psychologists (Ph.D.) are qualified to assess for ASD. Who can make an ASD diagnosis seems to differ state by state, but it is important to find a well-trained clinician to assess your child and to give an appropriate diagnosis and recommendation.

ASD can be diagnosed by the age of 18 months. Some children may be diagnosed much earlier but a significant number of children with ASD show typical development at first, and then lose those abilities by 18 months. Parents notice their child's developmental differences earlier when the child has ASD with intellectual disabilities, daily support needs, and speech language delay. However, developmental differences among children with higher intellectual abilities may become evident only once they enter preschool where circumstances require more social interaction.

More detailed discussion of the diagnostic evaluation and intervention is found in Chapter 2.

ASD Core symptoms

Regardless of the complexity of autism and how each individual presents symptoms differently, there are two core symptoms of autism outlined in DSM-5. Identifying and understanding the core symptoms, as well as any co-occurring symptoms, is central to helping you decide which therapies and IEP accommodations to advocate for your child. Note that not all of the following symptoms are present in each individual, and many other symptoms co-occur very frequently.

1. Social communication / social Interaction issues- Children with autism often avoid eye contact and do not look at you when their names are called. They may like playing alone and show no interest in other people. Even children with autism who appear to be interested in communicating often have difficulties carrying out a conversation. They may talk with enthusiasm about the topics they are interested in, but do not understand how little other people are interested in the topic. For this reason, they may struggle in pragmatic social communication.

2. Restricted and repetitive patterns of behavior, interests or activities-Some children with autism may play with toys by lining them up, without the imaginative play that typically developing children engage in. They like to repeat the same activity or schedule and get upset when the pattern is interrupted. Some children like to pursue their interest in minute detail.

Sensory needs and differences are also a part of these criteria. Sensory needs are the need for high sensory input or, conversely, need for avoidance of sensory contact. People with sensory differences may process the information that they take in through their senses (touch, sound, sight, taste) differently than TD people. For example, the people who need high sensory input often find deep pressure from a weighted blanket can make them feel calm. Others may feel that a soft touch is painful and avoid any contact. Still others may feel overwhelmed when too many people are present because they are not able to filter out some of the sounds, making it impossible to concentrate on one voice. They might experience the same reaction to overwhelming variety of sights or smells.

I personally feel the differences in sensory needs should be a separate category but it is true that those needs restrict the autistic person's daily life in much the same way as do other restricted and repetitive patterns of behavior. Please also refer to Sensory Differences in Cognitive Differences below for more information.

Autism Spectrum Disorder and Co-occurring Conditions

1. Difficulties in **Social communication and social interaction**

2. **Restricted, repetitive patterns of behavior, interests or activities.**

3. **Intellectual disability** (Mild to Profound). 50%-70% of individuals with ASD also have low IQ of 65 and under when Wechsler Intelligence Scale (WISC) is used to measure IQ. Scores between 90 and 110 are considered "normal".

4. **Language impairment**- the individual may not able to talk and may require communication devices.

5. **ADHD/ADD (Attention Deficit, Impulsivity, and/or Hyperactivity) and/or Learning Disorders**

6. **Co-occurring medical conditions**. For instance, as many as 1/3 of autistic individuals may also suffer from epilepsy.

7. **Sleeping and eating difficulties.**

8. **Anxiety and Depression** are often present among people with ASD.

Levels of Support Needed

Depending on how people are impacted by ASD and other related symptoms, they are assigned a level for the amount of support they need.

Level 1	Requiring support
Level 2	Requiring substantial support
Level 3	Requiring very substantial support

Some people need help for self-care and simple daily care (Level 3), while others may have genius level IQ but still require support for social interactions (Level 1). People with Level 2 are somewhere in-between.

Similarities and differences in individuals with autism

Below are some example descriptions of children diagnosed with ASD. Each example shows some core symptoms and co-occurring issues. These individuals have been fictionalized.

- Jeff is an 8-year-old boy. He appears to be bright and talkative. Once you engage him in conversation, you soon notice that he keeps talking to you in animated detail about what he is interested in. He does not notice that you are not particularly interested in what he said. Other children often exclude him and make fun of him as Jeff is not able to play cooperatively and gets angry when others do not play in his way.
- Anne is 4 years old and likes playing alone. She could spend hours drawing animals. At her preschool, she likes to sit away from the circle time and gets upset when other children accidentally touch her arm. Her parents are puzzled when her preschool teacher talks about her concern. Anne is an only child and she never bothers others and willingly follows her parents' directions at home.
- Tom was not able to talk until age 3. He goes to speech therapy weekly but it is hard for him to express himself like other 9-year-olds. He likes making everything correct, so he erases his writing frequently when there is some mistake or imperfection. His same age peers do not care much about how their hand writing looks. He also has difficulty focusing on his tasks and takes ADD medication daily.

- Angie is a 14-year-old girl. She does not like going to school. She says that school is "stupid." She especially dislikes group work and she is very shy around other girls. She does not know how to be a part of groups. She thinks that everyone makes fun of her. Angie says that she does not care what other girls think about her, but it is obvious that she still is interested in being accepted by others.
- Stephanie is a 4-year-old girl. She is impulsive and has difficulty sitting in one spot. Her language is limited so it is hard for her to make her needs known. She shows no interest in playing with others. She seeks interpersonal sensory input, often by throwing things and hitting others.
- Thomas is a 13-year-old boy. His special visual skills are extraordinary and he is good at putting puzzles together and understanding math problems. However, when he has to speak up in the class, he struggles to make sense. He is not good at writing, coming up with ideas, or organizing his thoughts. Thomas is frequently anxious and worries that he may make mistakes or not understand what he supposed to do.
- Sarah is an 11-year-old girl. She has limited spoken language and is often more interested in things more age appropriate to preschoolers. She also has problems with motor coordination. When she gets frustrated, she often screams and forcefully grabs things to express how she feels.
- Jason is a 4-year-old boy. He likes patterns and dislikes it when his schedule is changed. He is also sensitive to noises and dislikes sticky textures. He struggles to fall asleep and often wakes up in the middle of the night.
- Anthony is an 8-year-old boy. His visual IQ is in the genius range. He understands math and geometry at much higher levels than his peers, but he has little understanding of how others think and is not good at explaining his ideas in ways that others

understand. Consequently, he gets frustrated when others do not understand what he is thinking. He throws tantrums and sometimes kicks and hits others.

- Edie is 6 years old. He can realistically draw many animals from memory. He can also tell you what day of the week your birthday was on 20 years ago. He gets very upset when he perceives that he has made a mistake. When he becomes upset, it takes a long time for him to calm himself down.

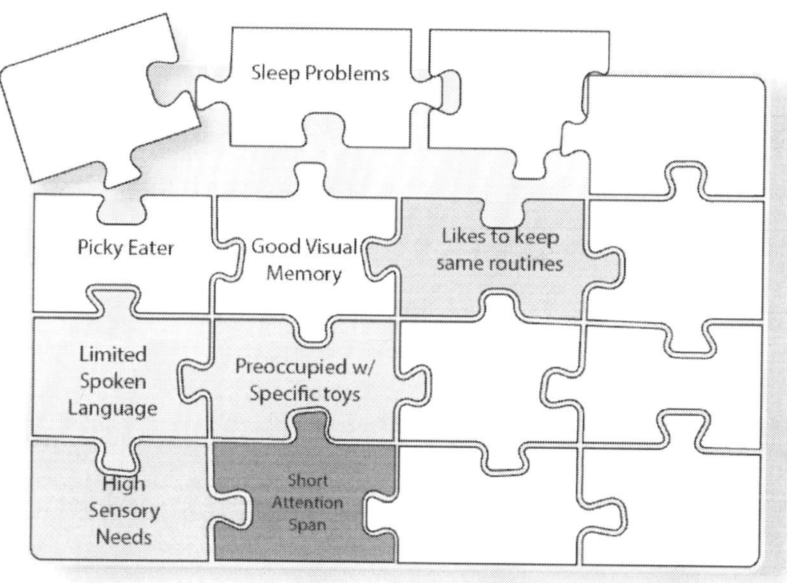

Figure 3: Autism puzzle

The illustration of a puzzle (Figure3) showing how different traits and issues fit together to help you understand your whole child. The autistic symptoms are shown in light gray and the occurring conditions are in dark gray. The white puzzle pieces are other characteristics that affect how the child functions daily.

Recent changes in diagnosing autism

When DSM-IV (the previous edition of Diagnostic manual) was published in 1994, ASD was categorized under Pervasive Developmental Disorders. Autistic Disorder was the main diagnosis and Asperger's Disorder and PDD-NOS (Pervasive Developmental Disorder Not Otherwise Specified) were the diagnoses that were used to describe individuals who did not meet all of the criteria for Autistic Disorder, but many people with Asperger's and PDD-NOS were considered somewhat autistic (Figure 4).

When DSM-5 was published over 14 years later in 2013, the diagnostic community decided to eliminate the following from the category of Pervasive Developmental Disorders: Asperger's Disorder, PDD-NOS, Childhood Disintegrative Disorder, and Rett's Syndrome. Before DSM-5 was published, the treatment community began using the term Autism Spectrum Disorders (plural) in place of Pervasive Developmental Disorders and also used the term "high-functioning autism." However, neither term was used in DSM-5 (See Figure 4). I wondered what would happen to people who had been classified with Asperger's Disorder and PDD-NOS. In 2015, I began to hear of some people being denied services at school because they did not have a diagnosis of ASD. In my practice, I have not witnessed any children being denied services already provided through an IEP (Individual Education Program) at their school because their diagnosis is not ASD. I have been told that it is best to revisit the clinic that gave your child the Asperger's Disorder or PDD-

NOS diagnosis to reassess your child to find out if she or he meets the criteria for ASD. DSM 5 itself notes that the individuals with diagnoses of autistic disorder, Asperger's Disorder and PDD-NOS should be given the diagnosis of ASD. However the individuals with the marked deficits in social communication but whose symptoms do not otherwise meet criteria for ASD should be evaluated for Social (pragmatic) Communication disorder.

Recently I heard from a parent whose child had a diagnostic evaluation at a well-established clinic. The clinician still talked about diagnoses from DSM-IV, the previous edition of DSM. This child's diagnosis, as well as my experience with other diagnoses suggests to me that DSM-5's simplified definition of autism does not always explain the whole spectrum of autism. It is also possible that some clinicians prefer having more ways to classify clients. When the DSM next revises the manual, it is likely that clinicians will discuss whether there should be a different diagnosis for people that do not meet the criteria of ASD, but still struggle in the area of social communication under the umbrella of autism. I am not sure if anybody is getting Social (pragmatic)Communication disorder diagnoses and what kind of treatment or support are available for the individuals with this diagnosis.

People with a diagnosis of Asperger's Disorder in DSM-IV often struggle to fit in social groups and have strong interests in certain topics and objects. They often call themselves "Aspies" and some do not like to be considered autistic. When Seattle's leading research hospital ran an advertisement to "cure diabetes and autism" some people with Asperger's felt insulted because they are proud of being "Aspie." They feel that even though they may be different from typically developing people, they do not have a disease to be cured.

Even though Asperger's Disorder is no longer in the psychiatric diagnostics manual, I often see individuals with autistic traits who are not diagnosed as having ASD. Some of these individuals might benefit from having a specific diagnosis. Many of them have difficulty understanding that other people have separate thoughts and feelings, and many struggle to read social cues. They use expressions that hurt other people's feelings. For example we do not say, "Your nose is big," even though it may be true because we know that comment may cause hurt feelings. However, individuals with Asperger's or limited social communication skills tend to think it is OK to say what they think or what is true. If they say what they think and are not aware that they hurt other people's feelings, soon they are excluded from social activities and teased for their behavior. They are often anxious and not sure why they sometimes make other people angry or are excluded from social activities. They need to recognize their differences and seek professional assistance to learn coping strategies.

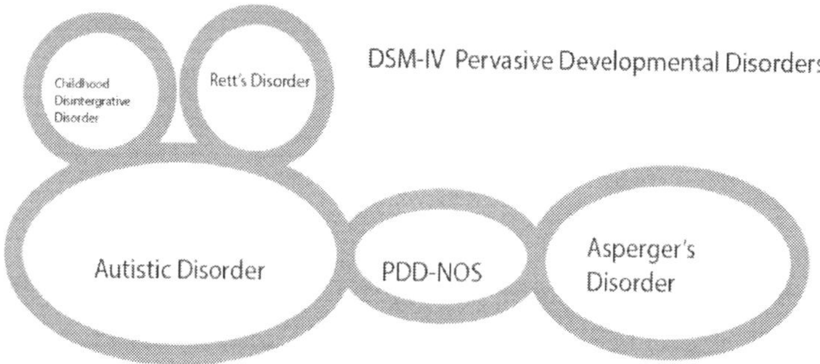

DSM-5 Definition of Autism, co-occuring disorders and Broader Autism Phenotype

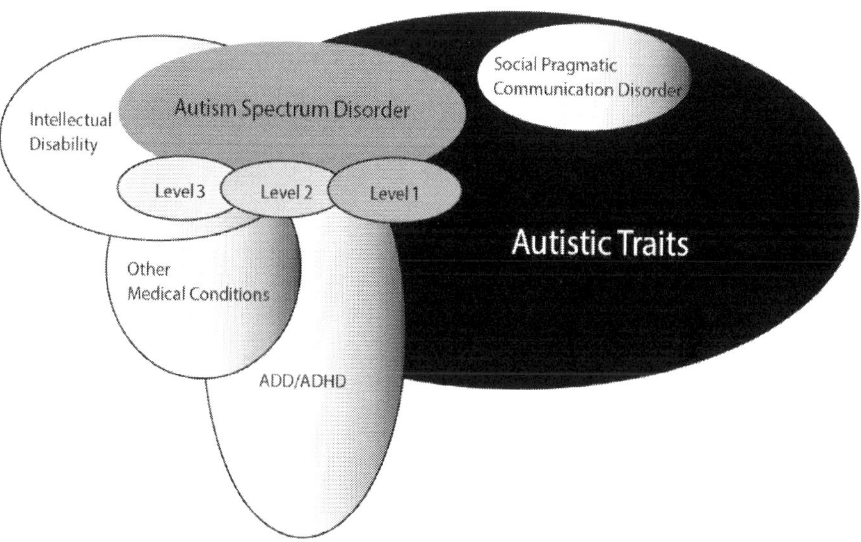

Figure 4: Autism diagnostic changes from DSM-IV to DSM-5

Gender Differences

Currently more males are diagnosed with Autism Spectrum Disorder. The nation-wide autism support group Autism Speaks website notes that "Boys are nearly five times more likely than girls to have autism. (2009) ". The ratio of boys vs. girls with Asperger's is 10 to 1. Some researchers, such as Dr. Simon Baron-Cohen, hypothesize that autistic brains function more like extreme male brains. Dr. Shana Nicols, the author of *Girls Growing up on the Autism Spectrum* said "the girls slip under the radar. Their autism looks different." She thinks the diagnostic clinicians use the scales that made for males. The females with ASD without intellectual disabilities are often shy and learn social interaction through playing with dolls and being looked after by other girls when they are younger. However when the girl reaches adolescence, the caregiver girls move on to find their own social groups and the girls with ASD are left alone.

I work often with girls with high-impacted ASD and very limited language skills. Among the girls with autism, it is much easier to identify the ones with low IQ and classic autism than it is with boys.

I volunteered at a local autistic girls' support group and met some high functioning autistic girls. They have caring and concerned parents who sought help early. They have more boyish personalities and tend to act out. In my practice, I see ostensibly typically-developing teenage girls who seek treatment for high anxiety and depression. They present autistic traits without an ASD diagnosis. They often are withdrawn and have social difficulties, but may not act out at school. It is possible my observations are biased by my hyper awareness of autistic traits, but I think there are undiagnosed girls who do not get early intervention because they do not disturb the classroom. They stay isolated and quiet, which our society expects girls to do, resulting in under-reporting of autism in girls.

Getting help for teenagers itself is challenging enough, helping teen girls with undiagnosed autism is even harder. They have learned to be isolative, without a clue how to socialize with other girls, and are often rejected by peers. They often fail to see how their behavior affects other people's views. It is very important to diagnose autism early in girls. By identifying their differences, they can learn to have positive social interaction with others.

Cognitive profiles of people with autism

Learning how any brain works is very complex even without adding in the complexity of autism. To further complicate matters, the brain evolves with human experience. There isn't a brain scan to diagnose ASD because there is no typical autistic brain.

Temple Grandin, PhD, a well-known animal behavior scientist and autism advocate, volunteered to take a number of brain scans to try to understand the autistic brain. In her book, "Autistic Brain" (2013), she found some structural differences in her brain but she points out that her brain and the brain of another person with autism may not be identical.

Instead of studying brain scans, clinicians focus on an individual's cognitive profile. While DSM describes autism based on its symptoms, cognitive styles tell more about how the people with autism process information differently. A cognitive profile describes how your brain functions on a daily basis. For example, how quickly you process information and how you solve problems affect you individually. You may prefer solving problems visually or by using language. Your tendencies to see one event logically or emotionally changes your perception of the event itself.

Current research is working on identifying cognitive profiles of people with ASD by observation and by administering standard tests. When a person is diagnosed with ASD by trained professionals, a cognitive profile can be created. Both verbal and nonverbal IQ and adaptive skills are assessed. Each person with ASD has a distinct cognitive profile. Very often people with ASD show more uneven results with broad cognitive split than typically-developing (TD) people. For example, people with ASD may achieve a high score in visual testing but a much lower score when the tests require more verbal problem-solving skills. Chapter 2 has more information about how and what kind of tests are administrated when people receive a diagnostic evaluation.

Genetic researchers have been trying for decades to find genes that cause autism. Other researchers look at how the brains of people with autism develop, such as connectivity, social motivation and social cognition. Genetic researchers have found up to 1000 mutated genes associated with ASD and it appears that there may be several different disorders or at least several types of autism. Currently we know the cause of about 10 % of autism, such as fragile X chromosomes, Rett's Syndrome and Tuberous Sclerosis.

Because autism is so complex, perhaps instead of finding your child's autism genes, it is better for you to discover your child's cognitive profile in order to understand how his/her brain naturally functions and what kind of therapy goals might be beneficial.

Cognitive characteristics often seen among people with ASD

The information in this section is not based on scientific experiments or tests. Rather, it is based on my own qualitative observations and those of other clinicians. The exact functioning of a typically-developing brain still presents a mystery to researchers; therefore it may not yet be possible to know how autistic brains function differently. Nevertheless, the following represents an effort at creating a cognitive profile for a person diagnosed with ASD.

Social interaction and sense of self (Mindblindness)

What I observe in most individuals with Autism Spectrum Disorders in my practice is a failure to sense boundaries and relationships between self and others. Dr. Simon Baron-Cohen hypothesizes that "Mindblind" people (autistics) are blind to other people's minds or emotions. This issue is of tremendous importance regarding relationships with family members, speech-language development, early learning, and the ability to form friendships.

The ability to maintain eye contact is often something young babies with autism do not naturally have. They may not look at you when they are called by name. You may wonder at first whether your child does not hear you very well. Once a test rules out hearing impairment, you may feel that you are totally ignored when you need his/her attention, but the child will pay attention to you when they have needs to be met. This is very often the thing parents notice first and when they begin to suspect some problem.

A young child with ASD has difficulty understanding that people around them are there not only for "me." An early indicator that an infant may have autism is when a child does not point at the thing in which he/she is interested. Instead, he holds his parent's hand and guides the hand to what he wants to have. He pulls the parent's hands to get what he wants, as if the hand were his. The sense of "self" physically extends to others around him; there is no difference.

At the age when a typically-developing child begins to talk, some children with autism may show language impairment; some may not be able to talk at all. Some may exhibit echolalia which is the repetition of another's speech. In many conversations, understanding depends on reversing the subject from you to I. Reversing the subject must be hard to do when you do not recognize the boundary between self and others. When your child's speech therapists work with his/her speech, they are not only teaching them how to talk, they are usually working on social interaction as well.

Even among the most verbal individuals with autism, many either do not participate in conversation at all or they have one-sided speech instead of a back and forth conversation. They may not care if others are interested in what they are talking about. Many of them also struggle to understand social cues. Some people with autism do not understand that other people cannot hear what is in their mind. They might expect others to understand without talking to them. For them, the thought in their head is as real as a verbalized thought, so others should understand it as well.

As a point of comparison which emphasizes how distinct each individual with ASD is, I have also met someone who is extremely sensitive to others' needs and emotions. She appeared to be anxious, as it is difficult for her to read social cues, so she works extra hard to figure out what other people expect from her.

Local Processing Bias/Weak Central Coherence

Local Processing Bias describes the tendency of a person with ASD to process information in a non-associative fashion. Generally when information is received by sensory input from your whole body, you need to organize and generalize the idea based on various inputs. What you see and what you hear might be slightly at odds, so the brain must adjust the information to a coherent concept that makes sense of the disparate pieces of information. Individuals with autism tend to over focus on the detail of just one input instead of integrating all inputs into one concept. This way of processing information may cause literal interpretation of language, a black-and-white simplistic thinking style, inflexibility, and an inability to understand symbolism and abstract concepts.

It is often difficult for a child with autism to transfer a skill learned in one setting into another setting. Their tendency to process information in a non-associative fashion makes them very literal and concrete thinkers. For example they can practice social skills such as taking turns in social skills groups, and learn to do the right thing every time in that controlled environment, but they may not able to apply the skills on the playground as they play different games with different peers than the social skills groups. Their intense interests and perseveration, (the obsessive need to learn details and collect information) may be related to the detail-oriented nature of Local Processing Bias.

Local Processing Bias helps a person to focus on details and to profoundly understand subjects where there is strong interest. This cognitive style could help those with ASD to specialize and succeed in specific fields such as math, science, engineering and art.

Sensory Differences

As humans, our five senses connect us to our world. We may assume that everyone has similar perceptions, but this is not the case among people with sensory differences. A visually or hearing impaired person certainly interacts differently with the world around him than a person with the five senses intact. It should not be surprising that a person whose brain processes sensory input differently would also interact differently.

Each time I start working with a new client I realize how each person gathers information in his own way. Most people like to look around and touch things. Some may be anxious because they do not know me, the environment, what is expected. When upset, some require sensory input with weighted stuffed animals or cushions with various textures, while others can take a very short time out to calm down. Each person appears to crave a structure they can rely on.

Aspects of sensory differences

Texture and touch

People with ASD may be very sensitive to the texture of clothes and being touched by others.

Hearing

People with ASD may perceive sounds as being louder, or more intrusive than TD people. They may struggle to block out background noises.

Sight

Autistic people may see objects differently and be more sensitive to light. Some may be hyper-vigilant to environmental changes and over react to the changes.

Taste

Frequently children with ASD are picky eaters. They may struggle to swallow bigger pieces of food, and they may also be overly sensitive to the texture of the food.

Visual IQ and nonverbal vs. verbal tasks

Individuals with ASD often show higher scores on nonverbal tasks than verbal tasks. This may be obvious among the nonverbal individuals, but even those with good verbal skills often excel in visual IQ. I have seen an evaluation for a middle school age child who showed college level visual IQ with early elementary school level verbal IQ. This is an extreme difference but it is very important to understand the differences between visual and verbal problem solving skills, so we can support the child according to his or her learning style.

Visual and spatial abilities

Many people with ASD process information visually and are good at seeing the details in visual images. They may excel at seeing the patterns of several objects. These characteristics are detailed in Chapter 3.

Executive functions

Executive functions are a set of cognitive processes and are also known as cognitive control and supervisory attentional system. Executive function is like the CEO of the brain. It's in charge of making sure things get done from the planning stages of the job to the final deadline. . Those skills also help us to get along with others and learn and study in the school systems. .

People with ASD may struggle in these areas:

1. **Inhibition**. It is difficult for them to wait and see what will happen.

2. **Attentional Control**. Children with ASD may overly focus on an object or a subject that they are interested in and are not good at shifting their attention to other tasks, even when prompted by adults.

3. **Self-Monitoring and Emotional Management.** It may be difficult to recognize their own emotions as well as the emotions of others. Some individuals struggle to recognize facial expressions. Managing emotions mean that you recognize the emotions and express them in social appropriate ways. It is more difficult if you do not recognize it in the first place.

4. **Initiation**. Children with weak task initiation skills may freeze up because they have no idea where to begin.

5. **Working Memory**. This is the child's ability to hold information in her mind and use it to complete a task. Kids who have weak working memory skills have trouble with multi-step tasks.

6. **Planning/Organization**. They may struggle to make a plan without clear guidance.

Individual Personality

To create a cognitive profile that is useful, it is important to understand each individual's personality and to realize that not all difficult or unique behavior is due to autism. Many of the behaviors we label as "autistic" are present at times in Typically Developing (TD) children as well.

Prevalence and of autism and causes

According to the Centers for Disease Control and Prevention (CDC), about 1 in 68 children has been identified with ASD. The first time the Autism and Developmental Disabilities Monitoring (ADDM) Network researched and published the prevalence in the year 2000; this ratio was 1 in 150 children. The newest number published in April 2014 is based on research in over 11 communities throughout the United States on children who were 8 years old at that time. The community studied in New Jersey had the highest rate, 1 out of 45.

We do not know the exact reasons for this increase, but the previous diagnostic system using DSM-IV (which included the diagnoses of Asperger's Disorder and PDD-NOS), significantly contributed to the identification of more people with Autism Spectrum Disorders (plural). The establishment of standardized diagnostic system also may be one of the reasons for increased identification. Identifying the children with autism helps to start early intervention but because autism is a spectrum disorder, it is still hard to understand (and broadly debated) how many core symptoms you need to have in order to be identified as having the disorder instead of a simpler collection of traits.

Two main theories regarding the cause of autism deal with genetics and environmental factors. It is beyond the purpose of this book to go into details on these theories. If you are reading this book you likely have already been touched by autism as a parent, a friend, a grandparent, a teacher or a student, and have been or will be referred to other sources.

Because of the increased prevalence of ASD, researchers tend to focus on identifying genes and creating subtypes of heterogeneous autism. Early identification and interventions on the younger siblings of the children with ASD are well established. Some people talk about the prevention of autism among the people who could be vulnerable to autism.

Lorna Selfe, in Nadia Revised (2011), pointed out the irony of Local Processing Bias (over-focusing on details) among autism research communities. She described the "field of autism research, which all too often seems a fragmented tapestry stitched from differing analytical thread of theoretical pattern."

As a counselor in a position to assist the parents to work through the process of diagnosis of autism, referral to appropriate intervention and school placement, I believe that we need to see the whole picture of the autistic individual instead of the detailed and fragmented information. I accept each individual diagnosed with autism as a whole person; unique and special.

Figure 5. Puzzle Worksheet

Write down your child's autistic traits and difficult issues to solve the unique puzzle. Please refer to Figure 3 on page 12.

Chapter 2

From Diagnosis to Early Interventions, and Beyond

Why is diagnosis important?

The simplest answer is so that you can receive maximum early intervention for your child. Getting an ASD diagnosis as early as possible, and starting treatment when your child's brain is actively developing and plastic, gives your child a better chance to catch up and learn the skills he or she needs to thrive in our society or in the Typically Developing (TD) world.

Once a formal diagnosis is made, your child is able to receive special education services as needed in the category of autism under the Federal guideline of the Individuals with Disabilities in Education Act (IDEA). Recently more insurance companies have started covering these costly therapies, but you need an autism diagnosis by qualified professionals in order to access the therapies.

As I discussed previously, autism is heterogeneous, and people with ASD range from those who are severely affected, to those with only a few ASD traits. It is possible to find many people who have ASD traits, but who do not have an ASD diagnosis. People with special talents and a supportive environment may overcome difficulties associated with ASD, even without the diagnosis and the subsequent treatment. However, that is rather rare, and the majority of undiagnosed adults with ASD struggle as they are growing up. The diagnosis gives many adults a sense of relief. Finally, it is clear to them why they had social and other difficulties when they were growing up. While early intervention is a must, I think it is never too late to get the diagnosis, so you can start coping with the condition and start accepting and loving yourself.

Overcoming the "why not wait" attitude

It is unlikely that a child with autism will outgrow autism without intervention. Over the last 20 years, I met many children without ASD diagnoses in the classrooms where I worked. Some parents felt their children were enrolled in a good program and did not think much about their children's future. Some were afraid. 20 years ago, autism was very much an unknown condition and it was scary. Pediatricians did not know much about Autism Spectrum Disorder(s), so they told the parents to "wait and see." One school or program with talented teachers can provide the best possible intervention for your child in early childhood, but when your child gets older, they will need different professionals. Children's needs change as they get older. Children with diagnosable ASD do not outgrow their conditions. In my experience, the differences between children with diagnosable ASD and TD children get wider as they get older.

The oldest child I ever sent to a formal evaluation was 10 years old. His parents absolutely refused to have him evaluated despite the fact that he was being teased, bullied, and rejected by his peers. He had above-normal IQ with a strong and restricted area of interest in science. His parents believed that having a diagnosis or a disability meant no future for their son. The proper intervention was to help him work with the difficulties and gain a chance to thrive using his special talent in science. It took me 6 months of counseling sessions to convince his parents to go through the evaluation. Based on the formal evaluation, his school developed his Individual Education Plan (IEP) and he started receiving much needed support at school. His IEP helped him to attend a social skills group and practice his learned skills on the playground with peer support monitored by his special education teacher.

It is in the best interest of your child to overcome the fear of diagnosis, and to learn about ASD and intervention.

Standard autism diagnostic tools and who is qualified to diagnose

In the state of Washington, trained psychologists, neuropsychologists, neurologists, developmental pediatricians, and child psychiatrists are all qualified to diagnose people with autism. I suggest searching for professionals who are trained to use the four basic tools (standardized tests) listed below. Please refer to the specialists in your state regarding the diagnosis process.

Diagnostic tools

WISC The Wechsler Intelligence Scale for Children (WISC), also called an IQ test, assesses an individual's cognitive abilities. It measures verbal comprehension, perceptual reasoning skills (visual), working memory, and processing speed.

ADI-R (Autism Diagnostic Interview-Revised) is a semi-structured, investigator-based interview that caregivers use to obtain an individual's developmental history.

ADOS The Autism Diagnostic Observation Schedule is an unstructured play assessment, a direct evaluation of social communication skills and observation of restricted/repetitive behavior by qualified and trained professionals.

VABS-II The Vineland Adaptive Behavior Scales assesses communication, daily living skills, socialization, and motor skills,

I personally prefer assessments by trained psychologists/neuropsychologists since the evaluations not only confirm or rule out autism, but also give a brief cognitive profile of the individual (read about cognitive profiles in Chapter 1). Ideally it is best to meet with a team that includes an MD, a psychologist, an occupational therapist, and a speech language pathologist. That way you will have a more comprehensive understanding of the individual with ASD.

The parents' conference after evaluation

The conference after the evaluation is the time to understand your child's needs. It is vital that professionals who evaluate a child for ASD spend enough time for family members to ask questions, get feedback, and receive recommendations.

Understanding the individual jigsaw puzzle of your child's cognitive profile and autistic characteristics is VERY important for starting treatment and receiving the correct school intervention. Always ask why your child behaves in the manner they do. Be specific about behavior you have observed. It is possible that your child did not exhibit the behavior while the professional was observing. It is very likely that every single unusual behavior has a reason behind it. The evaluators may not have immediate answers, so it is important to keep asking.

Neuropsychological evaluation

In addition to the diagnostic psychological evaluation, a neuropsychological evaluation can help you to better understand your child's cognitive profile.

I often recommend that my clients seek a neuropsychological evaluation when the children have co-occurring conditions that interfere with academic progress and social interaction. The neuropsychologists apply standardized tests to understand the child's executive functioning (noted in chapter 1) and other learning difficulties to determine the child's individual needs.

What is high functioning autism?

The term high functioning autism is often used to differentiate children with ASD from children with lower intellectual abilities (formerly called mental retardation). DSM-5 differentiates autism using three levels of support needed, and does not use the terms high vs. low functioning.

In my experience, individuals with ASD who have higher intellectual abilities (sometimes even with genius level IQ), experience different challenges from the individuals who need day by day self care and support. For example, one 9-year-old boy with limited language may still be working on toilet training, while another 9-year-old talks exclusively about an animal he is interested in, talking in great detail, without noticing that nobody else is interested. Nobody wants to play with him because he is not able to catch a ball, hold a conversation, or interact in a game. He may be excluded, while the first boy may be warmly accepted as a child with special needs.

I use the term high functioning autism in this book to discuss basic IQ differences because I have not been able to find a commonly understood alternative term. The term "ASD with IQ of within or above normal range," is too long, and "low-impacted ASD" is unclear. I say this to emphasize that "high functioning" does not mean that a child does not need specialized support, it means the level of support and kind of support is different for individuals with high functioning autism.

English as a second language and ASD diagnosis

When an individual's primary language is not English, it can become difficult to diagnose or rule out ASD. Most facilities affiliated with hospitals provide trained interpreters for the assessment.

When individuals have highly-impacted autism, clinicians do not hesitate to diagnose them with Autism Spectrum Disorder. Assessments using language interpreters can become challenging however, for individuals with minimum support requirements, or who have what was formerly called Asperger's Disorder, or those with autism and average to high intellectual abilities, since a core symptom of autism is concerned with communication and language.

If your bilingual child receives an inconclusive result, you may seek a professional who speaks your child's primary language or may have to wait few more years for your child to become more fluent in English. If you choose to wait, it is best to seek treatment and whatever school intervention that your child could receive based on their behavior without a formal diagnosis.

ASD Diagnosis and its impact on family members

Qualified evaluators are good information resources for families of children who receive an ASD diagnosis. Some evaluators offer treatments after the evaluation, while others give you a list of places you can contact. Moving forward after a diagnosis can be difficult for family members. You may still be trying to digest your child's diagnosis when you have to start time consuming and very intensive early interventions. You are told that you have to start as early as possible. Accepting your child has "disabilities" is itself a very difficult process. Raising typically developing children is challenging enough. Each child has different personalities, skills, strengths and weaknesses. In addition to all those challenges, your child has the difficulties associated with ASD.

Your child might have had a typically-developing babyhood and then began losing their babbling cheerfulness after their first birthday. Perhaps your child gradually withdrew and seemed to go backward in language skills. This happens fairly commonly. It is often discouraging to watch this happen. You see something of the spark inside your child, but he or she seems trapped and unable to come out.

From denial to acceptance

When we face high stress events, such as loss of a loved one or a major diagnosis of illness, we often go through five basic stages before accepting the condition. We at first deny the fact, then we get angry, we feel guilt and wonder what action or inaction we did to cause this, we get sad or depressed, and then finally we accept the fact. This is not an easy process, and we may not move forward. Typically we go back and forth between the stages. This idea was first proposed by Elizabeth Kubler-Ross in her 1969 book *On Death and Dying.* The important thing is to understand we all need to go through the same process, at our own pace, toward acceptance. It is OK to feel the way you feel right now.

Self care and support by non-judgmental others

Once you feel comfortable enough with the ASD diagnosis, it is important to build your own support system. Many people do not understand autism or why your child behaves in certain ways. Educate yourself and then educate your family members and friends. Remember that you do need time away from your children sometimes. Having understanding and accepting grandparents and friends is a necessity. Taking a child with ASD to a playground and other public places can be challenging and you may isolate yourself to avoid strangers' criticizing eyes. Creating a supportive team with your spouse, partner, extended family members and friends can help you to take care of yourself and regain the energy to go through the often arduous school negotiation and ongoing therapy sessions.

Support Groups

I started a group for parents whose children have developmental disabilities about five years ago. A majority of members have children with ASD. We meet four times per year, provide childcare, and the therapists, teachers and advocates are all invited. Interspersed with these meetings, we have play dates, parents' yoga, lunch, Christmas parties and fundraising activities. Now I co-lead the group with two other parents and two professionals. We have around 40 members, with a mixture of parents, professionals and volunteers.

Over the years, the group has had ups and downs. One time the group was taken over by pessimistic ideas and victimization. I felt that the pessimism was contagious and once we got infected, we were stuck. What helped us move forward was to re-introduce positive ideas and gradually we began empowering ourselves.

In the Seattle area, Seattle Children's Hospital Autism Center has family coordinators with many resources including support groups. Local schools PTSAs also have groups specifically designed for parents who have children with special needs. There are a lot of advocacy agencies who can direct you to the group you are looking for, including The Arc of King County. It is not difficult to search for local parental support groups through the internet and I hope you can find one to meet your needs. Many advocates and leaders of parental support group have their own experience with children with special needs and understand what you go through.

If you do not find a good support group, you can create a group with other parents. Invite the professionals who are working with the other parents to share their perspective.

It is hard to have a child with special needs. We cannot deny it, but taking it one day at a time with a mindful, positive approach will help you to move on and find the best path forward.

Some parents have ASD or autistic traits

If you yourself have ASD or autistic traits, you may feel that what is going on with your child is rather normal and it may be hard to accept the idea of an autism diagnosis.

It is important for you to understand your own traits and how that impacted your life. I strongly suggest you separate your experience from your child's experience. As I have mentioned, autism is heterogeneous. Every case is different. Your needs and your child's are different.

You might have struggled when you were growing up without supportive and understanding professionals around you. Since then, we have made tremendous progress to understand ASD and autistic traits. The way you were treated by the professionals in the distant past may not apply to your child's case.

Sibling care

It is hard for non-autistic siblings to accept the autistic sibling's needs and accommodate them. Parents tend to prioritize the autistic child's more immediate needs in order to get optimal results. Do not fall into this trap; siblings can be tremendous help for you. Make sure you are regularly spending some special time with your non-autistic children.

Are evidence-based treatments the best option?

If you search the internet for "Autism Treatment," you will find thousands of different treatment options. This is likely because we do not have a simple guaranteed treatment approach that works for every single person with ASD. ASD is a complex disorder with limited known cause and without proven tests based on blood, genetics, brain scans or other physical diagnostic tools.

A report from Frank Porter Graham Child Development Institute at University of North Carolina at Chapel Hill, (2014)

Evidence-based practices for children, youth, and young adults with Autism Spectrum Disorder, discusses evidence-based intervention and the most effective, scientifically researched interventions for ASD. To say a treatment is evidence-based means the treatment methods have empirical evidence of outcomes that are academically accepted by many researchers and universities. For example, researchers may hypothesize that a treatment works for children with ASD and above average IQ. They compare the children who get the treatment and the children who get a different treatment over certain period of time. The children's results on standardized tests are measured and compared before and after treatment, to ascertain which group made more progress.

Often I see a treatment modality which is not listed as evidence-based, but I know from firsthand experience that the treatment has worked on several children. I do not exclusively recommend treatment modalities based on an "evidence-based" label. I have seen acupuncture reduce anxiety in one of my clients, but this may not be the case for others. Eastern medicine, such as acupuncture, is difficult to evaluate using Western scientific methods. Eastern medicine has over 2000 years of history but it may not have enough scientific research to call it evidence-based. Just as in any other field, the skill of the therapist will greatly affect the outcome of the therapy. I find some therapists who are talented and good at engaging a child and some who are not naturally aligned with their clients.

Which therapy or intervention should you choose for your child?

Below are my recommendations for parents and family members with a child newly diagnosed with ASD. Remember that each child is unique, and will have a different way of experiencing ASD.

School

I usually tell parents to start the school evaluation while waiting for the diagnostic evaluation. In the state of Washington, if your child is under 3 years old, you should contact your local "Birth to Three" program which provides early intervention. If your child is older, contact the school district where you live. This may differ state by state, but in the Seattle area, many services are funded by local government and many are free of cost. The school district does not diagnose your child, but evaluates your child's development and skills and, if qualified, your child can start the intervention there.

There are two different ways to get support at school. One is an **IEP** (Individual Education Program), and the second is **504 Plan.**

IEP Individual Education Program

> The school district uses a team of professionals to identify areas where the child is struggling and creates a plan to support the child at the school. Depending on each child's needs, he or she could receive the following services:

Classroom behavior support
Academic support
Organizational support
Occupational Therapy or Physical Therapy
Speech Therapy
School based Social Skills Groups

In order to be qualified for an IEP, a child needs the following:

1. Diagnosis of disability.
2. Determination that the disability results in "adverse educational impact."
3. Determination that the child requires specially designed instruction.

When you advocate for your child at school, make sure you are talking about #2. Having an ASD diagnosis does not automatically mean that the condition has "adverse educational impact" according their guidelines. Understanding both the school guidelines and the recommendations of outside professionals (such as diagnostic providers, speech therapists, occupational therapists and child psychiatrists), could help your child to get the support he or she needs to thrive at school.

Once a child is on an IEP, the child's progress is monitored and the team meets annually to review the goals. He or she is re-evaluated every three years in the state of Washington. Recently I saw an amazing re-evaluation done at one of our local school districts. The child got his ASD diagnosis about three years ago. This year he was evaluated by a team consisting of a school psychologist, his preschool special education teacher, his current regular classroom teacher, a speech pathologist, an occupational therapist, a physical therapist and the school nurse. It was amazingly thorough and the child continuously received comprehensive support; such as access to support staff while he attends the mainstream classroom, specially designed small size classroom, and individual weekly occupational and speech therapies.

504 Plan

A 504 plan provides accommodations and modifications for a child with a diagnosis made by medical professionals outside of the school districts. Typically that means that the school districts accommodate but do not provide direct services, such as one on one speech therapy and occupational therapy services. Just like students with an IEP, the school teams meet with the parents and review the plan annually. The school does not evaluate your child.

Interventions outside of the school

Behavior. ABA (Applied Behavior Analysis) and ABA related interventions have high rates of progress in reducing challenging behavior and helping individuals with ASD function more like typically developing people. ABA is defined as the process of applying behavioral principles to change specific behavior while re-evaluating the effectiveness of the intervention. Many preschools for children with special needs utilize ABA therapy and the parents hire outside ABA therapists to provide up to 40 hours (recommended at least 15 hours) per week direct intervention.

Speech therapy helps to improve core symptoms of communication difficulties. Trained speech pathologist should be able to help nonverbal children to learn to use AAC (Augmentative and Alternative Communication) and PECS (Picture Exchange Communication Systems). The speech pathologists also work on pragmatic social communication skills.

Parent Implemented Intervention. Parents should be guided by teachers, ABA therapists and/or speech pathologists to learn strategies to help the child with ASD to function daily. The professionals should be able to guide you to use the visual schedule and social stories to reduce difficult daily behavior while at the same time understanding the reason behind the behavior. The visual schedule uses a picture format to help your child to understand what will happen ahead of time. The professionals could make a story book to teach your child what is expected in a certain situation and what he/she might do in that situation in the social stories.

There are many applications available for phone or tablet computers to create a visual schedule and visual aids.

Pivotal Response Training (PRT) is based on ABA and Parent Implemented Training and was developed by researchers at University of California at Santa Barbara. They have an online course to learn the method. PRT builds on a child's initiative and interests, which makes it particularly effective in developing communication, play and social behavior.

Sensory integration (occupational therapy). Research in this area seems to show mixed results in its effectiveness. It provides for a weekly sensory therapy to balance the child's sensory issues such as over- and under- sensitivity to stimuli. Please refer to chapter 1.

Occupational therapists utilizing Sensory Integration also work on fine motor skills.

Social skills groups. Children with ASD often have difficulties generalizing the skills they have learned. This means they might learn rules and turn taking in the social skills groups but they may not be able to go to recess and apply the skill in the other setting. It is better to help them to practice the learned skills in the natural settings without close supervision by adults.

Teaching peers how to guide ASD children and practice on the playground can be effective as well. Practicing social skills on site without direct adult intervention is effective for ASD children. For older children, there are the social learning applications you could use on your tablet or computer.

Counseling (psychotherapy). Cognitive Behavior Therapy (CBT) helps people with ASD to identify negative and ineffective patterns of thoughts and behaviors and to replace those thoughts and behavior with alternative and functioning ones.

I strongly suggest that parents of children with ASD get some form of their own counseling or family counseling to understand ASD and its impact on themselves and their families.

Alternative health

Bio-Medical Naturopathic doctors can test your child's food allergies, and need for minerals, vitamins and enzymes. A local Naturopathic doctor also gives immunization shots with an altered schedule to children with ASD. Gluten and casein free diets have not been proven to be effective for all ASD people, but balancing the diet and having healthy digestion is beneficial for everyone's physical and mental health, regardless of condition.

Body Work. Many holistic treatments originating in Asia, such as acupuncture and acupressure, work on the whole body balance. I have seen a child with classic autism receive acupuncture without using needles. She calmed down after treatment. A parent reported that neurological chiropractics helped her son to reduce his anxiety and other difficult behavior. I recommend, if you are interested in any type of holistic bodywork, do your research and ask other parents to find out if it could be a help for your child.

Lifelong interests-music, art, science/math club, sports etc. Based on their individual interests, I strongly suggest adding an activity that your child really enjoys. This will help them come out of their world and willingly relate with others. Music therapy is a well-researched treatment modality to help people with ASD increase communication. Many individuals with ASD like and excel in music. Some children may be good at math, science and computers. Others are good at art. Those activities may lead them into a career, but also help them to feel proud of themselves and to be motivated to socially interact with others.

Multi-system approach-create your own support team. You generally need to become your child's case manager, coordinating school and other outside therapists. No matter which treatment options you choose, it is important that all modalities are integrated and helping your child as a whole. In an ideal world, I think your child would receive most of the treatment at school, such as academic support, ABA and behavior intervention, speech and social skills, music therapy and art therapy as well as an after school program for science and chess club as a part of their IEP program.

Art therapy. I will talk intensively about art therapy and autism in the next four chapters. In short, art therapy is not art class. Art therapy can help your children to increase their autonomy, communication and to reduce ASD core problems. Art therapists need to be art teachers, so ideally your child can learn to use art media effectively. This modality may not be effective for some individuals with ASD. Art therapy could be used as a part of counseling and CBT, as a relaxation activity and as play therapy, which is considered an intervention with promising and emerging evidence according to the research conducted by Lindgren and Doobay at University of Iowa (2011).

A gentle reminder for parents

The journey of living and teaching your child with ASD often becomes a very lonely one. Often even with two involved parents, one of them becomes the primary care giver who stays home, negotiates with the child's school, takes the child to therapy sessions, and so on, in addition to usual daily housekeeping jobs.

This is a hard job that you should not do by yourself. You may encounter not only strangers in stores staring at your child throwing tantrums with a look saying that you are a bad parent, but also you may have plenty of your own family members who do not understand what ASD is and why your child behaves as he does. Please take care of yourself.

We cannot easily change how the whole world sees people with ASD, but you do need to educate your family members, neighbors, and friends, who can be your support team. Don't tell them that they should accept your child's difficult behavior because he or she has autism, simply tell them why they behave in that manner and what can do to help the child to behave in more socially accepted ways. In order to do so, you yourself need to know as much as possible, about why your child behaves that way.

Teenage years

Our body goes through a tremendous makeover during adolescence. Of course, this also happens among teens with ASD. I often hear from parents about behavior change among children with classic autism around that time.

Just like TD teens, we may have to closely monitor their changes, sexuality, social interests and desire to be independent, often with increased defiance.

My experience with high functioning teens with late diagnosis or no diagnosis but diagnosable symptoms has been very challenging. They come to my office to resolve their anxiety and social problems. It is hard to work with teenagers in general but the high functioning autistic teenagers are very difficult to engage. I think those difficulties are in part due to their unique cognitive profile with the inability to identify that other people have their own needs and feelings. They cannot see that their behavior is very difficult for others to accept. They may dislike some peers intensely without understanding why the peers reject them. The struggle to manage their emotions without early intervention is another challenge.

This is another reminder to not take a wait and see approach for evaluating children with the potential for an ASD diagnosis and to seek intervention as early as possible.

Life beyond childhood

Most parents of children with ASD work toward positive outcomes as result of treatment and school intervention. We face ups and downs as well as good days and bad ones during the process. Anything involving change requires time, consistency, persistence and hope. Current research shows that between 10 and 20 % of children with autism diagnoses lose the diagnosis as a result of early intervention, and intense therapy. This means that the child no longer meets the criteria for diagnosis and has learned alternative ways to function in the typical developing world.

This is a hard fact to face, but that means that 80 to 90 % of children with ASD still have ASD after they grow up. It is hard to hear stories where two similar children have the same intensity of treatment, and one has an optimal outcome and loses the diagnosis, while the other remains in need of a lot of daily self care support as an adult.

Research by adult autism specialists shows that by age 12 or

13, you may be able to observe what kind of future your child could have as an adult. Of course, we do not stop growing, and our brain's neuroplasticity exists beyond this age, but brain growth slows down around that time.

Regardless of your child's functioning level and progress, it is very important to accept who your child is. The first difficulty might have been accepting that your child has autism. The second one may be accepting, loving and caring for him as who he is.

Self awareness and being an advocate for oneself

Recently I heard from a parent with a 16 year old son with ASD about how the family created a transition plan starting at age 14. Based on his interest and future career choice, the IEP team chose high school courses. A vocational training team member joined his IEP and the son is planning to go to the training of his choice after graduating high school by age 21. In this particular case, his parent understands his abilities, strengths and weakness, and guided him to pursue a particular career choice.

Most parents create a comfortable environment for their children with ASD to achieve the optimal outcome to thrive in the neurotypical world. However, just as for any other TD children, it is important to empower them toward their independence in various degrees. I have seen some parents trying to engage their young adult sons to find work or go to school but they are too comfortable playing video games at home and refusing to move on to the confusing TD world. **Please do not wait until your child with ASD reaches adulthood to plan for their independence**.

Autistic individuals need self-awareness of their ASD and how it impacts their functioning in the TD world. This self awareness is dependent on their functioning level but in general they will benefit by being taught how to explain their ASD to others and how to get the support they need without you being solely responsible for advocating for your teen or young adult child.

If you have a child with classic, high impacted autism with low IQ, you may think that he or she will never become independent. Please remember there are different degrees of independence for each individual with ASD. Independence may include going to college, community college, or finding a trade or profession with and without help from vocational training centers. It could include attending day programs and pursuing something they will have a lifelong interest in, or could be living independently in a group home and participating in a community established to provide valuable and satisfying work for them. The potential is entirely up to each person's interest and ability.

Over 20 years ago, when a child got a diagnosis of autism, there was no clear guidance or treatment source. Parents recruited people to provide intense daily ABA therapy by themselves. Since then they have worked hard to get good resources at schools and communities. They are now struggling to find the resources for their adult children. By the time your child becomes an adult, those pioneering people might have established the resources for the adults with ASD. But I say again, please do not wait. I hope you join our advocacy activities to find good resources for our children's future resources.

Chapter 3

Art and Autism

I attend many ASD fairs and volunteer at parents' support groups. Everywhere I go, parents of children and adults with ASD tell me that they like art and they are good at art. In fact, research by Vital (2009) on over 6000 8-year-old children found that about 6% of children with ASD have noticeable drawing talent. This ratio is higher than TD comparisons.

There are books and websites devoted to documenting and advocating for artistic expression among people with ASD, even though art therapy currently lacks the research to be considered an evidence-based treatment modality for ASD. Nonetheless, in my art therapy practice, every day I see how children and adults with ASD enjoy art and learn new skills.

In this and the following chapters, I will discuss how researchers look at art among individuals with ASD, and how various aspects of ASD affect the art made by these individuals. By understanding those aspects, we will see that art can help people with ASD tremendously. Some people with autism naturally gravitate to art expression, discovering the healing power of art and learning to express themselves in pictorial forms which may be difficult to do in language.

Because there is limited research around art therapy as an

ASD treatment intervention, I also discuss other research related to art therapy.

Art and Cognitive Styles

In chapter 1, I discuss cognitive styles often seen among individuals with ASD. Here I am focus on how cognitive styles affect their art works.

Visual skills in intelligence tests

As a part of an autism diagnostic evaluation, the Wechsler Intelligence Scales (WISC-III) is commonly used to understand an individual's cognitive abilities and IQ. In WISC-III there are two main areas of cognitive abilities: verbal IQ, and performance (visual) IQ.

Researchers have noticed that people with ASD often excel in visually based IQ tests such as the Raven's Standard Progressive Matrices (RSPM). They also do better in the Block Design Test (one of the WISC-III subtests that is more visual in its testing method). Researchers investigating this issue tested people with ASD and non-spectrum participants and used participants from both groups that exhibited balanced verbal and performance (visual) IQ. Even though the researchers did not seek out individuals with higher visual IQ from either group, they still found higher scores in nonverbal skills in participants with ASD.

Local processing bias

As noted in chapter 1, local processing bias is the tendency to see the details instead of the object as a whole. As a deficit, people with local processing bias have difficulties organizing details from multiple inputs. Some researchers find similar tendencies among children with gifted realistic drawing abilities. Jennifer E. Drake conducted a series of studies (2010) on realistic drawing talent among TD children with artistic talent and children with ASD. She used the Block Design Task and the Group Embedded Figure Test as well as the Copying Task and concluded that skills in realistic drawing are associated with a strong local processing bias.

Because of artists' tendencies to see details, in higher art education you are actually trained to see the whole picture instead of details. For example, say you are trying to draw a person. You start the drawing as a stick or block image showing the proportion of the figure. You gradually add the curves of the figure, width of torso, a proportionally correct head, as well as legs and arms. You always compare each part of the body to the whole figure. You add more and finer details of facial expression, hair, fingers, knees and such at the end. You also are instructed to get up and see the whole drawing instead of sitting down and focusing on a small part of the object that you are drawing.

TD children develop abilities to draw more or less realistically around age 12, according to Viktor Lowenfeld (1949) in *Creative and Mental Growth*. Some children with ASD may gain realistic drawing abilities much younger than 12. It might be that their realistic drawing abilities come from different cognitive skills.

Some pre-teen to adults with ASD who have realistic drawing talents are able to see details and reconstruct that onto paper. They may draw in an interesting nontraditional order or may draw starting with the detailed hands and eventually complete the whole figure realistically by sequentially detailing the parts. Some may only see the details and struggle to integrate into a bigger picture such as a human figure.

At the same time this ability is correlated with their need for repetitive and restricted interests. They tend to repeat the same activity, which means that they practice the skills needed to create the image and have more opportunities to see more details each time they repeat the act. The repetition brings more joy in creating. These activities provide soothing and calming effects for everyone, not only for people with ASD.

Visual and spatial skills instead of verbal skills

People with ASD are often visually oriented. Temple Grandin writes in Thinking Pictures (1994), “One of the most profound mysteries of autism has been the remarkable ability of most autistic people to excel at visual spatial skills while performing so poorly at verbal skills.” She often talks about herself thinking in pictures in her various books.

In the research paper, Thinking in Pictures as a Cognitive Account of Autism (2010), Maithilee Kunda and Ashok K. Goel made a hypothesis, “A subset of individuals on the autism spectrum exhibits a disposition towards using visual mental representations,” (and a corresponding bias against using verbal mental representations) compared to the assumption, “typically developing individuals are, in general, able to use both visual and verbal mental representations.” This broad study showed significant evidence that certain individuals with autism may "think visually." However, given the heterogeneous nature of ASD, they were not able to generalize the idea. The individuals with ASD do well with the tests requiring more associative thinking, using pattern making and multiple choices such as Raven's progressive Metrics and Visual Search, Embedded Figure Task and Block Design subtests.

Not all the people with ASD are visual thinkers. In the forward to the book, Drawing Autism by Jill Mullin and Temple Grandin, Grandin writes "there are three different types of specialized autistic mind: visual thinker, the pattern thinker, and word specialist mind with no interest in art."

Grandin's idea appears to be supported by Kozhevnikov et al. (2005). Instead of the usual pairing of visual and verbal cognitive styles, Kozhevnikov et al. argues that there are in fact two distinct types of visual cognitive styles; object visualizers and spatial visualizers. She posits that some people are especially good at constructing vivid, pictorial and detailed images of individual objects, whereas other people excel in creating images that represent spatial relations among objects and in imagining spatial transformation. Object visualizers are thought of as having more artistic creativity, while special visualizers are thought of as having more scientific creativity.

Kozhevnikov did not apply her research to people with ASD but Dr. Grandin took Kozhevnikov's tests and found out she (Grandin) is more "object visualizer" with excellent abilities to look at the details of the object instead of spatial (pattern) visualization.

When I see individuals with ASD in the art therapy setting, I see both object visualizers who tend to get interested in details of the objects and spatial visualizers who are more interested in geometric shapes such as puzzles and origami folding. I think one individual may have both characteristics with the tendency to lean more toward one of them.

Interest in color

Regardless of each autistic person's functioning level in a cognitive profile, I notice many people with ASD have a keen sense of color. Some with strong pattern thinking like to create a color wheel. Nonverbal children with ASD also show strong preference in color choices. Related to this tendency, many children with ASD like to paint rainbows. They often know the exact order of the seven colors in a rainbow.

There are very few articles about color therapy and autism.

Hyperlexia and interest in letters

According to the Center for Speech and Language Disorders, hyperlexia is a syndrome that is characterized by a child's precocious ability to read (far above what would be expected at their age), significant difficulty in understanding and using verbal language, and significant problems during social interactions. They often can read aloud from a book but may not comprehend the meaning of what is written. Not all children with hyperlexia have ASD. Hyperlexic children are often fascinated by letters or numbers.

Many children with ASD like writing alphabets and strings of letters. They may be discouraged to do so in other therapy settings as it is considered repetitive and restricted behavior.

For art therapy, however, lettering is an important part of graphic art. In Asian children with ASD, I find many of them interested in their native language characters and letters as well.

Differences between creating and imagining

In the previous diagnostic manual, DSM- IV, one of the symptoms to meet the criteria of autistic Disorder was "lack of varied, spontaneous make believe play or social imitation appropriate to developmental level." DSM- 5 only says, "Difficulties in sharing imaginative play or in making friends; absence of interest in peers." These definitions are more about how children with ASD tend to play with toys in the social context. We certainly notice that many young children with ASD like to dump and pile or line up the blocks alone instead of building a house or imaginative place like their TD counterparts.

Both DSMs' definitions are rather vague and do not describe an area where I see individuals with ASD struggle. I find many people with ASD tend to stick with concrete and realistic visual images and ideas, and find it difficult to generalize images and ideas or create "unreal" ideas and images.

The British researcher, Dr. Simon Baron-Cohen categorized four different styles of play in his 1987 study:

1. Sensory motor-simple manipulation and/or sensual use of objects with no regards for their purpose.
2. Ordering-imposing patterns on the toys by

stacking-lining up.

3. Functional play-demonstrating knowledge of the appropriate functions of the toy.
4. Pretend play-substituting the objects for another by creating non-existing objects, attributing properties to the objects that were not real.

I think we could apply those styles to art creation as well. When we review the literature on imagination among people with ASD, we see many writers mix up the terms, "able to create" and "imaginative." It seems most people with ASD are "able to create." They try repetitively to draw what they are interested in, and the images are different from the original. I have seen quite a few children who can draw animals and insects in detail without looking at those images in person or in books. Some of them may be interested in comparing the sizes of the different whales on paper but have no interest in creating the ocean around, or any story involving them. This seems to be similar to the play they do when lining up the different blocks. So are they imaginative when they are drawing the whales?

Dr. Fiona J. Smith, in the Oxford Handbook of the Development of Imagination (2013), defines three aspects of imagination: visual imagery, pretense, and creativity. She thinks creativity requires "generation, manipulation, transformation of images to create novel presentation."

Research indicates that people with ASD, regardless of their cognitive abilities, show relative strengths in visual imagery, mental rotation of images and figure dis-embedding (finding a shape/figure within a bigger image.) Baron-Cohen researched (2001) how children with ASD and their TD peers created an "impossible figure." Unlike their TD peers, the children with ASD tended to struggle to make "spontaneous generations of impossibility."

In my practice, I meet children with ASD who love to create. They produce many art works and that makes their parent seek art therapy. Their creations, based on association and associated images, are often unique and original. Their art works appear to reflect the cognitive tendencies we seen among the people with ASD.

Each individual with ASD is unique, and the ability to create something imaginative and unreal also varies from individual to individual. Many individuals with ASD struggle to create something imaginative, or unreal. When playing with figurines, children with ASD tend to place characters in a line instead of making up stories in doll house play. Many art works made by individuals with ASD also tend to be limited in their interests, such as geometric patterns, alphabets, or characters in known historical events and characters from video games.

True creativity and imagination require someone to break the rules to conceptualize something that is not within the boundaries of what is possible or expected. This is often messy and involves the process of generating chaos and re-integrating that chaos. We may need to go through sensory experiences that lack clear patterns and that we may not be fond of. Often, individuals with ASD have greater difficulty doing that.

Art welcomes varied expression and does not discriminate

against people with or without ASD. At the same time, the artist creating visual art desires to be understood. Through art, they communicate their own thoughts to others. For people with ASD, art could be equally valuable for self-expression, but might also be a window for connection with others.

Artistic development in children

Among typically developing individuals, young children develop artistic skills gradually. Viktor Lowenfeld's work *Creative and Mental Growth was* published in 1947 and his theory is still relevant today. According to Lowenfeld, typically developing children begin to be interested in art when they are around one year old. They pick up a crayon and move it over a paper. They see the mark on the paper; they notice that they are responsible for the scribbling. They enjoy leaving the marks (not always on the papers!) and soon begin scribbling circles. The circles start having arms and legs and eyes that become their mommy or daddy. See Figure 6.

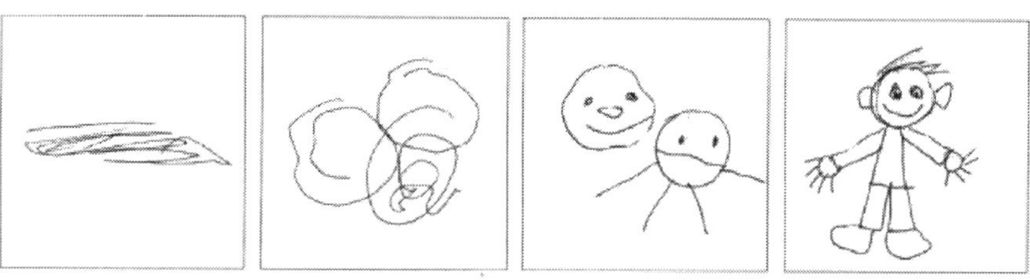

Figure 6: The developmental stages in art among TD children

Children with ASD may not follow the same developmental stages. Some with intellectual disabilities may remain in the scribbling stage. Some may not be interested in drawing humans and move to draw animals instead. Research by Nicole Martin (2008) indicated that the human drawings by the children with ASD lack details on their face drawings. Some children are capable to draw realistically much earlier than TD children without going through the developmental stages among TD children.

Repetitive interest in themes and images

Having repetitive interests is one of two core symptoms for an ASD diagnosis, and this is certainly seen in art works by people with ASD. This can be expressed as repetitive images such as alphabets, shapes, animals, daily objects, historical images, or really anything to which that individual is attracted.

Sometimes they repeat making images in order to create on paper a 'perfect' image that is in their mind. This behavior often causes distress since creating the near-perfect, almost computer-generated image by hand is a hard task.

Sensory integration issues

DSM-5 talks about Hyper- or Hypo- reactivity to sensory input or unusual interest in sensory aspects of the environment as one of the criteria for an ASD diagnosis. According to the Sensory Processing Disorder Foundation, (http://www.spdfoundation.net/about-sensory-processing-disorder) sensory integration dysfunction or Sensory Processing Disorder is the difficulty to accurately and coordinately process information received through the senses. Incoming information is processed by touch (tactile), proprioception (awareness of body position and input to muscles and joints), vestibular (awareness of head position and movement), sight, sound, taste and smell. The issues are often addressed in sensory integration therapy by trained occupational therapists. These dysfunctions greatly affect the art process and also affect vast aspects of one's daily life, and therefore need to be considered and incorporated into functional activities.

- **Tactile**

  When some children use finger paint, it appears to be calming for them. Some people with sensory cravings use paint in self-stimulating ways. However, using paint this way does not go beyond self stimulation without encouragement. It can be a slow process to transform an action from one of self-stimulation into one of self-expression.

  Some children, as sensory seekers, can be fixated on sensory-based objects or movements. These interests can be incorporated into creative activities. For example, there is a girl who likes balloons and she often carries around balloons. We used the inflated balloons to paint with. For a boy who likes saving small objects such as beads, the beads were replaced with precut paper shapes and it became a process of creative art work instead of self-stimulating and repetitive behavior.

  Some children are very sensitive to art media and dislike paints that stick on their hands. As long as they are engaged with art activities, they are very slowly guided to get used to the unfamiliar or unpleasant tactile sensations and are instructed to wipe their hands as soon as they finish using the media.

- **Body position and its awareness**

  Some children with ASD struggle with fine motor skills and creating an image can be hard. The playfulness of art making appears to ease their difficulties and helps them to work on practicing fine motor skills. However, art making requires a stable body; the artist needs the ability to hold the core of body as well as to move their arms and hands.

Calming effects of creating art and craft

Eye Movement Desensitization and Reprocessing (EMDR) is a therapeutic technique using bilateral eye movement and tapping tools to work on trauma. Making art may have a similar effect in that it connects the right and left brain as well as integrates other parts of the brain.

Art may also increase alpha brain waves and reduce beta waves to provide a balance of active and calming waves. Chris Belkofer (2008) conducted research regarding how the art making process changes brain waves. He found that art making increased Theta and Alpha waves, which are associated with calming and relaxing.

Dr. Jennifer E. Drake (2014), researched the regulating short-term effects of drawing versus writing. She concluded that, “Negative affect was significantly lower after drawing than after writing, even when the preferred activity indicated was writing. Participants were more likely to use drawing to distract and writing to express."In my practice, my clients voice feeling more relaxed and say the drawing exercises make it easier to identify the areas of life where they are struggling. I see that non verbal children with ASD enjoy the art activities and their difficult behavior is reduced.

Art reflects each individual's thoughts, feelings, personality and neurological differences

As an art therapist trained in psychoanalytical theory at New York University, and a practicing mental health counselor using cognitive behavior theory in the Pacific Northwest, I often try to bridge the gap between analysis-based and evidence-based theories.

Art reflects who you are and what you are thinking and feeling as well as subconscious and suppressed events, thoughts, and feelings. These elements also play a part in the art making of people with ASD. If you had a rough day, the line you draw may be more intense or weaker than when you are peaceful.

While drawing images and free-associating feelings and thoughts by looking at images are used as a part of standardized tests by licensed psychologists to understand the way our brains function, art therapists are not trained to use the same tests as licensed psychologists. Art therapists use standardized tests specifically developed for use in their work.

When I work with people with autism through art therapy, I

begin to get a glimpse of how they operate. I am not trained to assess how their physical brains function, but I can evaluate their fine motor coordination, visual abilities, eye hand coordination and thought processes as well as specific characteristics. There are psychological tests that may evaluate these functions accurately, but the art therapy community needs to develop evidence-based assessment tools to understand cognitive functions in the art creating process. The community will be served with additional understanding of how people with ASD create and how the creating process can be therapeutic.

Some individuals with ASD possess tremendous skills to see details and patterns, and also have the skills necessary to bring them to life on paper. We need to nurture their strengths and skills and help them to connect; otherwise these skills may remain trapped in repetitive, restricted and self-stimulating behavior. That would be a great loss.

How Art Can Help People with Autism

Simple spontaneous creative processes can be relaxing, such as playing with a piece of clay, doodling images on notebooks, or cutting shapes. During art therapy sessions, creating visual images helps people to understand their struggles, which are sometimes difficult to articulate with words. For people with ASD who have speech or language difficulties, visual expression is easier to understand than language. Sometimes introducing art activities to clients can lower their defenses, allowing them to become more cooperative in the counseling sessions.

In the book, *Drawing Autism*, a collection of art works created by people with ASD, Dr. Temple Grandin talks about how her mother nurtured her artistic abilities by teaching her and helping her "to create pictures that other people would want." The book shows many accomplished artists with ASD. Each artist also comments about how art is beneficial for them.

Jill Mullin, when she collected the art works by people with autism for this book, asked each artist, "What inspires/excites you about creating art?" Some artists were unable to answer on their own and the questions were answered by their caregivers. Their answers are:

- Sense of achievement and feeling proud of themselves.
- Focusing on their abilities instead of disabilities. They hope to inspire other people with autism to recognize their abilities.
- Feeling understood, accepted and validated by others without using words and increased desire to connect with TD people.
- Insight and understanding their own tendencies. Michael P. McManmon said he used to want everything to be perfect but once he started painting, he started, "to see things in a new perspective and I now see the beauty that I did not previously see, I decided that I can experience the world in any way that I want.

- Emotion management and feeling calm. Artists themselves recognized feeling calm as well as their caregivers observed the behavior changes. Some said art making process releases built up emotions.
- Joy and happiness in creating art.
- Sense of control and order. The art making process gives them autonomy and their own order out of chaos.

Just as typically developing children benefit from early childhood art activities, most children with ASD benefit from the art making process. I noticed their strong interest in art making but quickly found how they relate to art differs from TD children. Although many people with autism like art, it is very important to understand what the person with ASD gains from the activities. They enjoy the art works, but they may be self stimulating by using repetitive images or sensory media. They may dislike being taught different ways to do art and be unable to learn useful skills that could enhance their expression.

Chapter 4

Art Therapy as an Autism Intervention

In chapter 3, I talked about characteristics of art work made by people with ASD. In this chapter I will discuss how the creative process and art can function as therapy.

Even though many children with ASD show visual skills and preferences, that does not mean that all children with ASD excel in art making without guidance. Children with ASD may reject your guidance and resist changing.

By the time a child with ASD arrives in my clinic, they are usually exposed to drawing with pencils and crayons. These two tools are easily used at home and almost always available. It is easy to learn how to use pencils and crayons unless you have significant fine motor skill issues. But what about learning to paint? Painting involves learning how to use new tools effectively. Paint and water colors require more control and can more easily produce unwanted results. The unwanted results often lead to temper tantrums.

Artistic ability is often a strength for people with ASD, but helping them through art making can be challenging for parents and professionals. I hope this chapter helps you to help your child to overcome their obstacles, and that art becomes a tool to for them to communicate with others and feel proud of themselves.

Evidence and Creative Arts Therapies

Although art has been acknowledged and used therapeutically for centuries, the field of art therapy was developed in 1940's in the New York City area, where it was based on psychoanalytical theory. In the state of New York, art therapy is recognized as one of the creative arts therapies and the state licenses trained and qualified art therapists. The other creative arts therapies are music, dance, poetry and drama.

How art therapy is utilized in the rest of the United States depends on where you are. In New York State, art therapy is often used as a part of a multi discipline treatment team in a way that was more common before "managed care" hit the system. You will find art therapists working in hospitals, nursing homes, schools, wherever other therapies are practiced. Needless to say, NYC has a long history of being the capital of art and music. In Seattle, Washington art education itself is very minimal in elementary schools. The art therapy program started about 15 years ago and recognition of the profession and job opportunities in art therapy are very limited.

Unfortunately, the field of art therapy has been slow to produce research proving that it is an effective treatment modality for people with ASD. It lacks the quantitative data required and often the literature you find is only a series of case studies with limited research value. Even so, many people with ASD appear to like art making and websites like *The Art of Autism* (http://the-art-of-autism.com/) promotes their expression. While, as an individual clinician, I would like to see quantitative research in art therapy, sponsored at graduate programs, at this point, I determine art therapy's value on my thorough research on art and autism and on an individual basis for people who visit my clinic and trust my professional judgment based on my experience.

Educating and training art therapists

According to the American Art Therapy Association, art therapy is described as follows:

> Art therapy is a mental health profession in which clients, facilitated by the art therapist, use art media, the creative process, and the resulting artwork to explore their feelings, reconcile emotional conflicts, foster self-awareness, manage behavior and addictions, develop social skills, improve reality orientation, reduce anxiety, and increase self-esteem, among other goals. A goal in art therapy is to improve or restore a client's functioning and his or her sense of personal well-being. Art therapy practice requires knowledge of and skills in usage of visual art (drawing, painting, sculpture, and other art forms) and the creative process, coupled with application of theories and techniques of human development, psychology, and counseling.

As a minimum, art therapists must have master's degree in art therapy or a related field. After completing the master's degree, the Art Therapy Credentials Boards (ATCB) provides a strict guideline for art therapists to be credentialed to protect the public by promoting the competent and ethical practice of art therapy through the credentialing of art therapy professionals.

The credentialing processes are:

> The first-tier credential is the Registered Art Therapist (ATR) that requires specific graduate-level education in art therapy and documentation of supervised post-graduate clinical experience. An ATR then may apply to become Board Certified (ATR-BC). Board Certification requires the successful completion of the national examination, demonstrating comprehensive knowledge of the theories and clinical skills used in art therapy. An experienced Board Certified Art Therapist may also apply for an Advanced Supervisory Credential (ATCS). The ATCS is designed for professional art therapists who have acquired specific training and skills in supervision, and insures that supervised interns receive the best training available.

Currently, art therapists are licensed in the following states; Kentucky, Mississippi and New Mexico. Art therapists are licensed as creative arts therapists in the State of New York. In addition, art therapists are included in licensure law for counselors in many states, including in the State of Washington.

How art therapy is different from art education

Art therapists assess a client's strengths as well as areas that need to be worked on. They identify treatment goals and provide a nurturing and contained environment. We are artists, art educators, and psychotherapists.

In general, art educators teach people to draw more realistically or to learn how to manipulate the media differently, learning new techniques to foster expression. They value the finished art works. Art therapists have skills to teach our clients but we place more value our client's creative process. This means we may focus more on our client's communication through the creative process, reducing their rigid and repetitive interests through an ongoing developmental progression. When all aspects of the process work out, I find the final products of therapeutic art experience are very unique and beautiful, but that in and of itself is not the goal.

Nicole Martin wrote (2010), "Art is an interesting crossroads for children with ASD because it is an activity in which strengths (visual learner, sensory interests) and deficits (imagination, need for sensory control) emerge. They often desire art making very much but then have a hard time engaging in it appropriately."

How I work with individuals with ASD

The scenario below shows how art therapy could be used for an individual with ASD based on my experience and research. As each individual with ASD is unique with different support needs, it is important to create specific treatment goals for each individual. I hope this section helps you and your therapists to understand the complexity of the art therapy process and helps you find the best way for your child or loved one to thrive through artistic expression.

Information gathering

When I first get a referral, I gather information about each individual with ASD prior to meeting with them. I often request that the parent bring the original ASD assessment, IEP evaluation and current IEP goals. Some of them might have gotten additional evaluations by neuropsychologists, occupational therapists and speech pathologists as well before coming to see me as a mental health counselor or an art therapist. Ideally I see the primary caregivers, in advance, to talk more about their children's needs.

Preparation

My art therapy room is designed to eliminate unnecessary stimulation and distraction for my clients. Most art media that can be is stored in a cabinet and hidden from them until it is needed. The play therapy toys are in a cabinet with a very high door knob. This prevents impulsive children from opening the door and grabbing the contents of the cabinet. Some children are very fast and are good at noticing when I am not paying attention to them.

All children visiting my art therapy room for the first time are nervous. Typically Developing (TD) children get nervous when they visit new places, children with ASD are more nervous because they tend to dislike changes. I create a simple **visual schedule** to show them what we plan to do together as well as a clear behavior expectation chart (Figure 6).

Evaluation

I use a modified Kramer's Art Therapy Evaluation (1983). I simply ask the kids to draw, paint and use modeling media in our first session. I identify their developmental age in visual expression, fine motor skills, area of interests, areas of difficulties, areas of strengths and treatment goals.

Sessions

Based on the information from caregivers and the professionals and my initial evaluation, I come up with treatment goals (these are addressed later in this chapter). Based on the treatment goals, I prepare a visual schedule for them to follow in each session. Some children may like drawing and be very repetitive and restricted. I may place other activities for him/her to work on prior to the preferred activity.

Reward system

Until art making itself becomes rewarding for the child, I prepare small rewards between activities. The rewards are often various sensory toys while they sit and wait. Once they enjoy the activities, they are encouraged to wait or help to clean up.

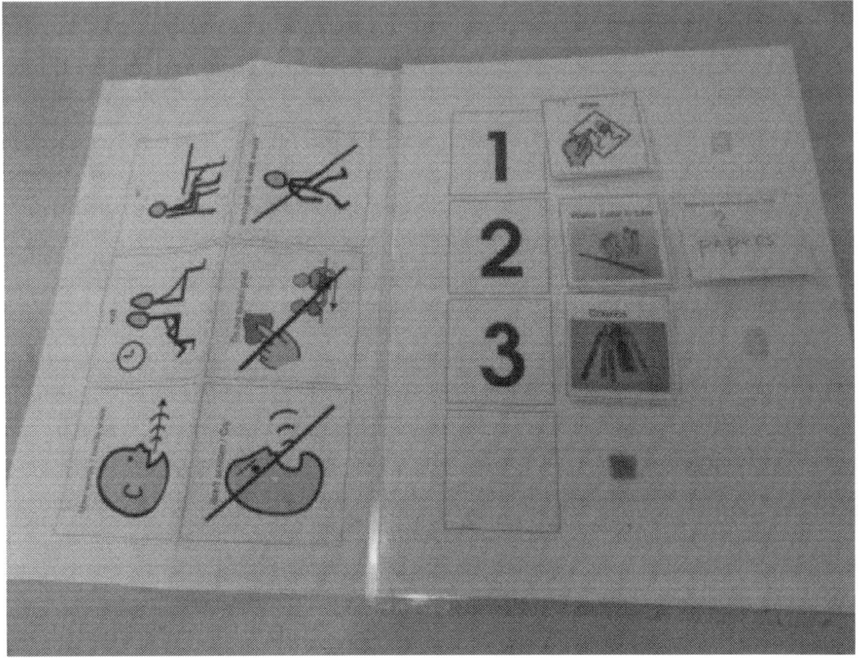

Figure 6: Sensory toys and visual charts

Handling tantrums

Even with all my preparation and evaluation, clients may whine and cry during the therapeutic process. The two main reasons for tantrums are to escape the activity they do not like, or to move to an activity they prefer. I do not give way, rather I help them to calm down or move on and distract their attention. I may guide them to move to a rocking chair with many stuffed pillows and animals until they are ready to move forward with the activity.

Establishing rapport

Establishing rapport with children with ASD is not easy task. They need to understand that I am there to help them to do what they want. At first they often perceive that I want to keep them from what they want. They want to continue doing what they want and are unwilling to try something new. Shifting their perception of therapy is hard but often it is achieved by having them express themselves in various art media. Changes should be encouraged but often need to be presented very slowly.

Once they learn my session structure, I begin altering the structure depending on each person's needs. I may introduce longer or different activities if their attention spans are much longer than the earlier sessions, and/or if they have learned to wait without sensory toys and other transition activities. They may have bad days but they begin enjoying art making even when they cannot continue their repetitive activities, accepting new ideas and developing good working relationships.

In this stage our communication and personal interaction sees huge advances during the therapy sessions, and communication through art itself. Children with limited language skills are encouraged to use a visual communication board and to use more words. At this stage, they are very much aware what is expected of them to continue the art activities and get help from the therapist. Impulsive children are also aware and try to wait and ask before grabbing art materials.

Various stages of art therapy process

I encounter children with diverse autistic symptoms and diverse age groups in my clinic. I describe below how I encourage children to create symbolic images in art works to share with other people.

☆ Some children may not be aware that if you pick up a crayon and move it on a piece of paper, you can make a mark on the paper. TD children start noticing this around 18 months of age. But children with ASD and intellectual disabilities may not have this hand/mind connection for creating scribbling, regardless of their chronological age.

They may like the sensory experience of certain art media but it is often self-stimulating activity. Still, their interest in sensory media can be a window for making intentional marks on the paper and progress to other art media.

☆ Some children may create scribbles and circles. They appear to enjoy the sensory input to their hand when they place the crayons and pencils against the paper. However, they may have no intension to make symbolic images. TD children in this stage may name the circles and scribbles as real life people and objects, even though the images may not resemble the named people or objects. Children with ASD tend instead to use scribbling skills for repetitive expression of shapes.

☆ Those scribbles and circles are usually developed into human faces and bodies among TD children. Among children with ASD, they may draw faces when requested, but the drawing often lacks detail and may not be spontaneous. They may prefer drawing animals and characters from stories and cartoons. They may like to create a list of the animals they are interested in and comparison of sizes. This may be related to their repetitive interest and pattern making.

☆ Once they can draw symbolic images, can they make a story or describe the relationships of the characters? When they make stories, most of them are reality based. I try to help them to broaden the story by changing and adding variation of the stories.

☆ When each person discovers their style and abilities to create art, the art accepts many forms of expression. As matter of fact, each artist creates images of the same subject that are different and unique. In this stage, I believe art becomes a bridge between isolative people with ASD and TD people.

Transforming difficulties into strengths

In this section I recount some case studies and discuss how to use art activities therapeutically, transforming potential deficits into strengths.

☆Repetitive and restricted interests

If a person with ASD likes art, art can be a window to open their connection with the rest of the world. It is easier to say than to do. Individuals with ASD often like to do art activities by themselves but are not always interested in being praised by others or offering reciprocating praises themselves. Their personal value of their expression may be different, and being praised for the works that they do not like (ex. not perfect enough) could be confusing for them. Repetitive and restricted interests are considered one of the core symptoms of autism and often are discouraged in many therapy and school settings. At the same time, those repetitive interests and behaviors can sooth their nervousness.

During an art therapy session, if a person with ASD likes alphabets, in art making, you may allow the person to "draw" all the alphabet letters with fancy fonts. This calligraphy could also be used successfully for graphic art designs.

Sam is a 9- year-old boy with limited speech. He likes to draw alphabets, usually with colored pencils. When given tempera paints, he tried to use paint brushes just as he did when he used the colored pencils. He was not able to accept the art therapist's suggestion to use more water or a wider brush to get the flow. He got frustrated and demanded more papers to start over. By limiting the number of papers he used during the sessions, Sam eventually accepted painting with a sponge roller over the alphabet that he disliked and started over painting new alphabets. I demonstrated how he could cover the original alphabets with the sponge roller beside him (Figure7). He understood that I was not preventing him from correcting his "mistakes" but I was showing him alternative ways for him to learn how to make the alphabet that he liked. This activity fostered a nurturing relationship for Sam to accept the therapist's help.

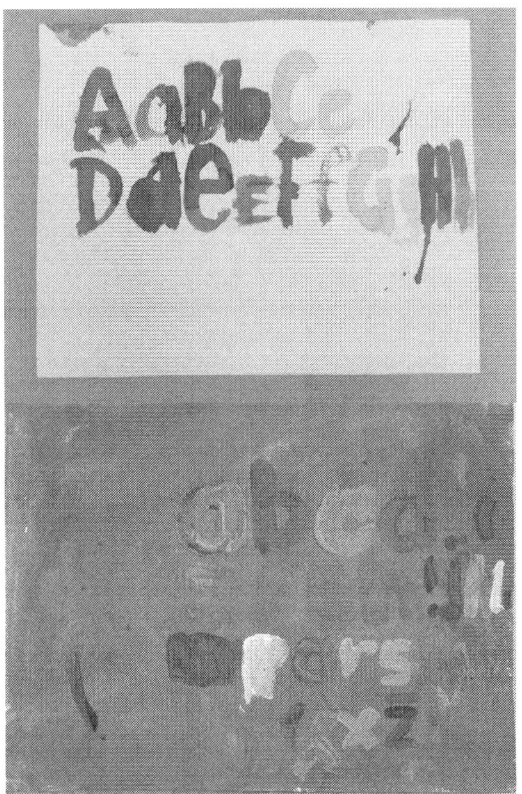

Figure 7: Original Alphabets pictures created by Sam (gifted to the therapist by his mom)

Ted is an 8-year-old with very limited speech. He likes to paint but he tried to use the paintbrush like the crayons that he was familiar with. At first he ignored my suggestion to dip into the paint instead of continuously rubbing the dry brush. Once he realized that I wanted to help him to achieve what he wanted, he began accepting my suggestions, such as using paint brushes of different sizes depending on the size of the space he wanted to paint, waiting for the paint to dry before he adds something on it, etc.

We also looked at various alternative images in Google

images on line, so he was able to draw and paint variety of images, instead of repeating the same ones. For example, he liked to paint a fish with human face. By observing the typical fish, he was able to draw fish with one eye when he drew a side-view fish image.

☆Imagination deficit

Imagination deficit is often described as one of the characteristics of autistic children's play. It is very common also in their art works. Not only are their art works repetitive but also their images often come from concrete images that they have seen and liked.

As I described in Chapter 3, Dr. Flora J. Scott, in the *Oxford Handbook of the History of Imagination* (2013) defined "imagination" as: 1. Visual imagery, 2. Pretense, and 3. Creativity (generation, manipulation, transformation of images to create a novel presentation). Children with ASD are often good at visual imagery. However, pretense is somewhat harder for children with ASD and this characteristic is noted within the core features of an ASD diagnosis. TD Children move sequentially from non-functional play to pretend play. Dr. Scott (2013) talks about four steps to reach pretend play: 1. Simple manipulation, 2. Imposition of patterns, 3. Demonstrating knowledge of the appropriate functional play, and 4. Substituting the object for other, created, non-existing objects and attributing properties that are not real.

Jessica was 3 years old when she started working with me. Her parents were concerned about her high anxiety, rigidity and frequent failure to engage in social activities.

She was referred to the appropriate clinic and diagnosed with PDD-NOS (Pervasive Developmental Disorder Not Otherwise Specified) and started early intervention at her school district. She could pretend to cook foods and eat them with play dough and cooking utensil toys, but she disliked playing with the doll houses. She found a polite way to decline playing with the doll house but soon it became clear that she struggled to come up with a story. TD children, including boys, typically love playing with the doll house. Boys may prefer using action figures instead of toy doll figures. For Jessica, playing with the doll house became a stressor. She struggled to understand and incorporate unreal stories.

In creating her art works, which was her preferred activity, Jessica repeatedly drew the same story based on her home life. In our sessions, we worked on developing different variations of stories through art therapy. By teaching her to vary the stories in her play, we prepared her to be less fearful of changes when she faces a new event..

☆Atypical developmental stages in art making

When typically developing children begin scribbling around 18 months of age, they begin with straight lines, first scribbling right to left, then progressing into circles. They begin drawing symbols for people, often at first one circle for a head and two arms and two legs sticking out of the head, without a body. Children with autism are much less interested in people and made up stories. I observe that they often draw animals and cartoon characters instead of the people around them.

Some children with classic autism and with intellectual disabilities may draw and paint like much younger TD children, often reflecting each child's developmental age.

Sarah is a 10-year-old girl who has limited spoken language. When she started working with me, she was impulsive and her attention span was very short. She scribbled with small lines and it appeared that she was not even aware that when she moved her hands in certain ways, she could manipulate the art media and make shapes she liked. After one year of sensory based art therapy, Sarah now intentionally makes circular scribbles, which are the next stage of TD development. How I worked with her is discussed more in the **Sensory needs** section.

Eddie is an 8-year-old boy with great visual memory. His mother reported that he was never interested in drawing people. She does not remember him scribbling much when he was younger. He is able to draw animals realistically from memory. His parents sought treatment due to his intense tantrums which would occur when he felt he had made some mistake. When he started working with me, he was interested in comparing the various sizes of whales. He only wanted to use lead pencil to draw and when introduced to painting, he was not able to control the media and he threw tantrums. We worked on how to accept the different media and to learn to accept mistakes and fix them through art making.

☆**Sensory needs** including self stimulatory behaviors

One of the criteria for repetitive and restricted behavior issues among children with autism is sensory issues. I am not sure why sensory differences are included in a behavior category, but their sensory differences, hyper- and hypo-reactivity are one of the characteristics of autism.

In art therapy, tactile experience can be both rewarding and challenging, depending on each child's sensory needs. Some may love smearing paint on their hands and arms. Some really dislike the art materials' stickiness on their skin. Learning balanced reaction to sensory experience is a key effort of sensory-based art therapy.

Sarah is 10 years old with limited fine motor skills. She loves finger painting but she preferred the paint on her hands and arms and was not interested in creating any lines with the paint. She was encouraged to move her fingers on the paper and enjoy paint and water. Eventually, she spontaneously moved her fingers and began creating lines instead of simple tactile self-stimulating.

Sarah also likes playing with balloons. She screamed when first I introduced the small not yet inflated balloons probably because she had only seen a balloon blown up before. She gradually accepted the balloons and she loves to paint with the balloons, with a much longer attention span and beautiful color choices. She eventually shifted to sponge painting as she was able to hold the sponges easier than balloons and she was able to make different marks with sponges.

Ted is an 8- year-old boy who loves to draw with crayons. His grip is very strong and the crayons give him the sensory input he craves. When he started working with me, he was introduced to working with oil pastels and paint. With the oil pastels, because of his strong grip he broke the children's oil pastels but the oil pastels for professionals worked well for him. I suggested that he use both the oil pastels and water colors because they are easier to control than paint. Eventually he learned to paint with water color without oil pastels. He still dislikes the watercolor sticking on his skin but now knows how to ask me to wipe it off or he himself wipes off the paint.

☆Gross and fine motor development

Many children with autism have deficits in both gross and fine motor skills. Regarding gross motor skills, in order to work with art media, you often are required to have core strength to hold up your body and your arms over time to handle various movements.

Art therapy can help people with ASD to learn to develop fine motor skills while enjoying art making activities. Please refer to Chapter 6 for art media and art activities to develop those skills.

☆Awareness of cause and effect (intent)

The creative process is much more complicated than we think. Some of the children who come to my office have little intention to create. They enjoy sensory experience of paint and clay but have no intent to create something in their mind. They may not at first even notice the mark your fingers make when you move your fingers on the finger paint tray. This was portrayed in Sarah's stories above. Art therapy can help children with ASD and intellectual disabilities to increase awareness of their body and their connection to their environment.

☆Object visualizers and pattern visualizers

As discussed in Chapter 3, Dr. Temple Grandin hypothesized two different kinds of visual processing cognition among individuals with ASD; Object visualization vs. Pattern visualization, in her book *Autistic Brains* (2013).

Object visualizers are good at seeing details and may be good at drawing things realistically. They may tend to focus on details and struggle to make connection with images as a whole work rather than a series of separate details.

Pattern visualization skills are seen among the people with good math and science skills. Those people are often also very good at writing computer code.

Depending on their individual abilities, you may want to encourage both object and pattern visualizers to use different art media.

Object visualizers could benefit from visual art instruction and encouragement to see the whole picture in relation to its surrounding instead of focusing on details, while at the same time fostering their keen abilities to see the details.

Pattern visualizers may like things like geometric designs, mosaics and origami with good instructions to copy at first (Figure 8). They often dislike doing artwork without guidance and appear to be more rigid, trying to do things their own way. When they are too rigid, they should be encouraged to accept imperfections and pattern changes.

Figure 8. Image based on shapes

☆Depression and anxiety

As I discussed in Chapter 3, creating art can be relaxing though there is limited clinical research behind it. I pose that a periodic shift from the verbal and complicated world to the visual and simplified world could help anybody, especially individuals with ASD, overwhelmed and over loaded in the modern world. Providing tool boxes of various visual and tactile activities could help all children to go through their stressful school lives.

Adults with ASD, especially those who have gone through their childhood without formal diagnosis and intervention, start counseling to deal with anxiety and depression co-occurring with ASD, or developed later as the result of social struggle and sensory overload. Unlike talk therapy, art therapy may help them to reduce anxiety and visually recognize their areas of struggle.

William is in his 40's with a diagnosis of Asperger's. The Autism (Asperger's) diagnosis was made when he was 35 years old. When he was younger, only classical autism was identified by the professionals. When he was growing up, he struggled to fit in and articulate his thoughts and ideas. Eventually he began believing that he was stupid and not good at anything.

The diagnosis of Asperger's gave him a sense of relief and we began rebuilding his self esteem, focusing on his strengths. Relaxing art activities, such as working with pottery clay, helped William to reduce anxiety when he talked about the difficult situations of his life and learn new copying strategies for each situation.

☆ Social communication issues

When children with ASD first visit my office, they are full of anxiety. They are curious about the art media in the room but they may withdraw into their own interests and ignore my presence. Some of them may touch everything in the room.

Our communication is usually visual. I demonstrate their options, different ways to handle certain art media, sitting next to them. They may continue doing their own repetitive creation but I know they are noticing what I am doing and when they accept my suggestion, we start our first step toward reciprocal communication.

At some point we begin establishing a rapport, which is different from talk therapy. They understand that I comprehend their needs and will help them to achieve what they want. When we reach this stage, we can move on. Once they develop the sense of trust we can start an interactive therapeutic relationship with increased communication and acceptance of new strategies for them to express themselves through art. During the art creating process, once therapeutic relationships are established, children with ASD and limited language skills begin practicing to make requests in full sentences instead of single words. At this stage, they are so engaged that they are more motivated to use words.

Jeff is an 8-year-old with a genius level of performance (visual) IQ. Despite his good pattern visualization skills, it was extremely difficult for him to see another person's point of view when we are talking. The picture in figure 9 is from an activity where we created an image together, and then verbally considered what the two clay people in the art work might need. First we each created a figure using cookie cutters, then we each gave something the other's figure needs, such as clothes and toys. You can see Jeff created a bone for the dog as well. I think this activity showed that he can understand other people' needs with the aid of visual and concrete (not abstract) figures of clay (Figure 9).

Figure 9: Play dough communication

Art as an alternative communication. Communicating by spoken language is often difficult for people with ASD. For some people, it is hard and frustrating to get their words out. Others may be able to talk but struggle to carry on conversations, not understanding social cues. The visual expression of themselves in art can be a welcome relief from the language-based daily life. Artistic expression also can become a window for them to visually communicate with the TD world instead of withdrawing into their world of art.

Art Based social skills groups can be beneficial to many people with ASD. In my small clinical setting, it has been difficult to find a good match to create groups. We need to find several children with similar difficulties, cognitive abilities and chronological ages. In terms of social skill groups in general, because of their difficulties in generalizing information, applying learned social skills in the group may be challenging for people with ASD. Research shows that learning rates for social skills are high in programs with coached peers.

Art Therapy Goals

These are typical art therapy goals for children with ASD with various developmental differences.

1. Increase intention/functionality of creating art , using the child's special interests such as tearing papers and touching balloons.

2. Transform sensory stimulation into a part of sensory-based art activities.

3. Obtain fine motor skills to make basic shapes such as circles, long lines and other shapes.

4. Learn to manipulate tools for drawing, painting, cutting,

gluing and modeling tools to create.

- Painting: different shapes, color theory, strokes and how to use varied brushes and amounts of water.
- Printing: use sponges and various textured objects.
- Drawing: find a media to accommodate the interest and fine motor skills.
- Modeling: learn to pound, push, attach, roll, cut and form modeling materials.
- Collage; tear papers, cut shapes and glue shapes, create with intention.

5. Develop ability to draw symbolic images such as animals, houses and people.

6. Make a story behind the art work.

7. Make non-reality based stories.

8. Increase spoken language during the art making process.

9. Increase interest and attention span in each activity.

10. Accept new ideas and decrease rigid and repetitive visual images and behavior.

11. Complete art work and feel proud of the art work.

12. Use activities that use the whole brain.

13. Relax and enjoy!

14. Create works that make them proud of themselves and that they want to share.

Art therapy goals as a part of counseling sessions

Art therapy is used as a part of counseling sessions for people without intellectual disabilities, so called high functioning people, with ASD. In addition to the above goals, we also work on

1. Identifying the source of confusion, depression and anxiety, and expressing that visually.

2. Increasing self-awareness; identifying their struggles and emotions related with ASD conditions and develops coping strategies.

3. Learning strategies to reduce anxiety and be calm, using various calming art materials.

4. Increasing social skills to use in their daily lives

Chapter 5

Autistic Artists

In this chapter I simply use the term "autistic artists" instead of "artists with autism" in an attempt to honor the concept of neurodiversity, which is about accepting all people with different neurological conditions for who they are.

In my research on autistic artists, three autistic artists stand out among the many: Jessy Park, Stephen Wiltshire, and Nadia Chomyn. They are all well known, and people are awed by their superior memories and ability to draw realistically. They may be called savants. A savant is a person affected with a mental disability who exhibits exceptional skill or brilliance in some limited field. Savants are considered unusual and supposed to not represent the general population of autistic people.

When I read and watched films about these three artists, I began seeing what affected them, and I took note of the elements that might be transferred to the autistic community as whole. I saw the fundamental theme of this book, accepting and encouraging diversity, helping them to thrive in a society not built for them and how they were helped by their immediate family members, professionals and their surrounding communities.

My research on autistic artists brought me back to Oliver

Sacks' writing. It was very inspirational to rediscover Sacks' work on autistic artists just before he passed away in late August of 2015. Oliver Sacks was a London-born neurologist who wrote essays on how the lives of people with various neurological conditions were affected. The essays do not simply recount the course of their "disorders." He observed people with keen clinical eyes, but also with incredibly warm and positive humanity. He wrote an essay about the animal scientist and autism advocate, Temple Grandin, in *An Anthropologist in Mars* (1993) when the general public did not know much about autism. Later, he wrote the foreword to Grandin's well known book, *Seeing in Pictures* (1994). When I first read his writing on autism, I felt his description of Grandin was rather offensive as he was describing her as if she were a different being. After I studied more on autism, I re-read them and was impressed by the accuracy of his observations and most importantly his commentary on how non-autistic people feel when they are with autistic people.

Oliver Sacks' observations were made when the majority of clinicians were not aware of autism as a spectrum disorder. In 1994, DSM-IV included Asperger's Syndrome in the manual and broached the concept that autism is a spectrum disorder and not everyone with autism is deeply impacted. Oliver Sacks himself had a condition often seen among people with ASD, prosopagnosia, which hinders his ability to recognize the faces of the people he knows. In his books, Sacks talked about his autistic artist patients: Jessy Park, Stephan Wiltshire, as well as José.

José

Sacks encountered José at Bronx State Hospital in the 1980's. "The Autistic Artist" was a chapter in *The Man Who Mistook His Wife for a Hat and Other Clinical Tales* (1987). José was labeled an "idiot" by the state hospital staff. He appeared not to talk nor understand what was asked, but Sacks asked José to draw as a part of his evaluation. Sacks said, "I nearly always ask patients, if it is possible for them, to write or draw, partly as a rough-and-ready index of various competences, but also as an expression of 'character' or 'style.' José drew a watch with details, which surprised Sacks, and he began encouraging José to draw. Later, José began showing his remarkable abilities to observe and draw in details and add his own characteristics.

Jessica (Jessy) Park

Jessy Park's mother, Clara Claiborne Park wrote about Jessy in *The Siege* (1967) and *Exiting Nirvana* (2001). When Jessy was born, autism was considered "Childhood Schizophrenia" and many autistic people were institutionalized. Their mothers were blamed for being "refrigerator mothers" as autism was considered to be caused by uninvolved and cold mothers. *The Siege* was about Jessy's early childhood and *Exiting Nirvana* was about life with Jessy when Jessy was in her 40's.

According to Sacks, C. C. Park wrote to Sacks after she read about José in *The Autistic Artist*. They made a documentary film, *Rage for Order* (1996) together, portraying Jessy and Park family members as well as other autistic people.

C. C. Park described in *Exiting Nirvana* how Jessy's artistic abilities were nurtured and that what motivated Jessy to paint houses (Figure 10) were the paychecks she received. She used to draw images other than houses such as electric blanket controls and heaters but she quickly learned that people prefer purchasing her pictures of houses. Money did not mean much to her but Jessy liked to see the numbers rise in her checkbook.

Park also talked about how her art works helped Jessy enlarge the social elements of her life. She enjoys praise and refreshment at her art shows, and makes commissioned works for her clients.

Figure 10: © Jessy Park (Source: Pure Vision Arts website) http://www.purevisionarts.org/artists/jessica-park/

Stephen Wiltshire

Stephen's amusing photographic (eidetic) memory and realistic drawings of buildings from memory were well recognized even when he was a little boy. Sacks' brother in London happened to be Stephen's physician and Sacks visited and traveled with Stephen to several different locations over the years. Sacks wrote about this experience in his essay, *Prodigies* (1993) in *An Anthropologist on Mars*.

The documentary film, *The Human Camera* (2008) follows Stephen's footsteps visiting his old school, and his gallery. The film shows Stephen flying over London for 15 minutes in a helicopter, and then drawing a panoramic view of London from memory, focusing on his amazing abilities (Figure 11). Sacks' writing on Wiltshire highlights how Stephen relates to other people; often Stephen is emotionally indifferent to the professionals who encourage him and recognize his abilities.

Oliver Sacks also described how Stephen changed over years, showing emotions, affection, and concern for the people that helped him. His later images are more creative, not exact copies of what he saw.

Figure 11: ©Stephen Wiltshire

http://tandfbis.s3.amazonaws.com/rt-media/pp/common/sample-chapters/9781848720381.pdf

Nadia Chomyn

Nadia Chomyn was an autistic artist who first was recognized and publicized by a British psychologist, Lorna Selfe. Nadia was born to Ukrainian parents who later immigrated to England. Nadia had speech/language and motor milestone delays, but was able to draw realistic horses with riders at age 3 (Figure 12). She primarily drew images from the picture books of the *Ladybird* series. She only drew from her memory with a fine ballpoint pen and drew continuously for up to one hour. She was referred to Clifton Day Special School at the age of 4 ½ . Her stunning drawing abilities were closely monitored. She later gradually lost her drawing abilities as she learned to talk, and began to copy other children's drawings when she reached adolescence. In *Nadia Revised: A longitudinal Study of an Autistic Savant* (2011), Selfe examined Nadia well into her middle age adulthood.

Figure 12: By Nadia Chomyn

Retrieved from http://discovermagazine.com/2002/feb/featsavant/

Temple Grandin talked about how much her own and Jessy's mothers encouraged them to create images that other people wanted. It appears that Nadia's mother encouraged Nadia to draw when she discovered her unusual talent at age 3. Nadia began drawing when her mother went through her own cancer treatment. When her mother died, Nadia was institutionalized. She seemed to have had art therapy sessions which did not help to continue her art work. It is not clear why she lost her drawing abilities or her interest in drawing but her connection with her mother may be one contributing factor.

Chapter 6

Engaging activities and art media

How to encourage continuous art experiences

Temple Grandin frequently talks about how important it is to engage children, adolescents, and young adults with ASD in activities that will help transform their so called "fixated" interests into built-in strengths, and sometimes even into a career. In *Thinking in Pictures* she tells us that all parents of children with ASD and professionals "should broaden it (fixated interest) into constructive activities." She talks about the science teacher in her high school who guided her to create her calming squeeze machine to reduce her sensory overload. In order to have that kind of impact, we really need to be understanding, creative, and imaginative.

Each person with ASD needs to be understood, accepted, and encouraged in order to thrive in the typical developing (TD) world. In this chapter, I discuss what kind of art activities and media help people with ASD continue their interest in art-related activities for their careers or hobbies.

Provide concrete and visual guidance

As much as possible, instructions should be concrete and visual. Language-based conversation is not a strength for most people with ASD.

Use a picture schedule and give clear demonstrations while working with a person with ASD to help broaden their interest.

Keep these things in mind when choosing activities and media

- Take note of daily and current health and mood.
- Cognitive style, physical abilities, and developmental age.
- Preferred media used for repetitive interests.
- Fine motor skills.
- Ability to understand cause and effect.
- Body core strengths.
- Attention span.
- Rigidity-think about how much they can tolerate when things do not go well.
- Ensure that you provide adequate time for transitions.
- Be ready to help when they get overwhelmed. Have sensory toys, weights, and rocking chair etc. sensory needs. This will affect how much water you allow. Many love playing with water but too much or too

little water could interfere with the art making process. Also note that glue sticks break easily and some may dislike the sticky glue on their skins.

Useful art media for people with ASD

You may think if you have paper and a pencil, you can create art. However, introducing specific media helps people widen their areas of interest and new media may help them express themselves differently. Help them to think outside of their boxes!

DRAWING

Some children with ASD have difficulty holding a pencil and creating images. Activities using thicker pencils and putting pencil grips on the pencils helps provide some control. I have also found that the consistency of drawing media impacts their control over the media.

Tempera color sticks—Sarah has Cerebral Palsy. It is hard for her to hold most drawing media except tempera color sticks. Tempera color sticks (Figure 13) are soft and paint-like. They are sold under various names and look more like markers but the colors themselves are more like pastel mixed with tempera paint and oil pastels.

Figure 13: Tempera color sticks

Stephanie is impulsive and has strong sensory needs. She likes nearly hitting the papers with art media. Crayons break easily and magic markers lose tips. The tempera color sticks are too soft and she does not like the crumbs that come out of the paste. We found she most enjoys drawing with oil pastels. They are not too hard nor too soft, but are just right for her.

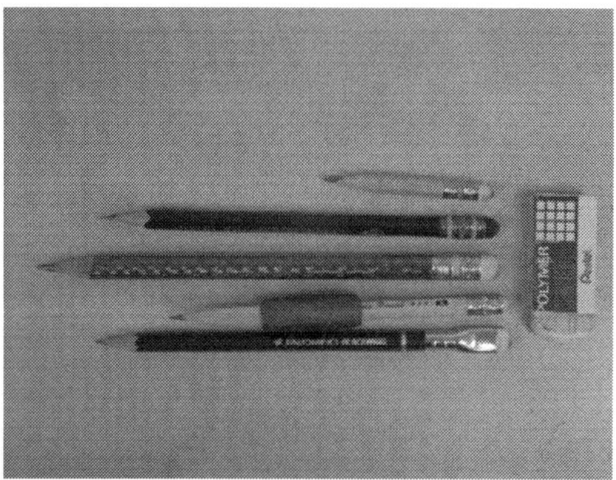

Figure 14: Various pencils and eraser

Pencils—soft, wider, triangle, thick, thin, long and short-Pencils with various sizes, lengths and blackness (Figure 14). I like B pencils because those are soft enough.

Erasers—Most use the small eraser on the pencils but plastic erasers are more suitable to erase drawing lines.

Colored pencils—I like softer, professional quality colored pencils with more color choices.

Crayons—I do not always use crayons during art therapy sessions with the people with ASD, but crayons are often a familiar material for them and I have them in my office so they can go back to crayons when other art media is too frustrating to use.

Figure 15: Children's and adult oil pastels

Oil pastels—Recently, I discovered that the slightly more expensive oil pastels (Figure 15) for adult artists are better than the inexpensive oil pastels that are made for kids. Many children with ASD are learning to control tension in their hands and have a tight grip when they draw and write. Some also enjoy the sensory impact when they press on the crayons and oil pastels to draw. The excess tension often makes the crayons and the children's oil pastels break, but the oil pastels made for adults do not break as easily.

Pens—May be used with teens, but not recommended if the person has limited fine motor control or likes to crush tips.

Chalks–Chalks are very easy to break, so this is for an individual who has good control and tolerates the dust from the chalk.

Magic markers- Magic markers could be alternative to other drawing media but the limited colors choices could limit their expression.

Teens with high functioning ASD may enjoy alcohol based bendable markers such as Copic markers.

PAPERS

- White letter-size all-purpose paper
- 12" x 8" white construction paper
- Colored construction paper
- Carson watercolor papers. This inexpensive but good enough water color paper helps people fix problems including wiping and painting over when they do not like the image or make mistakes.
- Tracing paper or layout bond paper. Tracing paper helps them learn different ways to draw instead of sticking with their repetitive and restricted images.
- Card stock
- Finger paint papers

PAINTING

- Finger paints—I use tempera paint and mix with liquid starch (Purex, Sta-Flo) instead of pre-made finger paint.
- Tempera paint
- BioColor paints (Figure 17)
- Various sizes and shapes of paint brushes, rollers and sponge brushes
- Dry watercolors in trays

- Liquid watercolors
- Sakura Koi Water colors in tubes (Figure 16)

Figure 16: water colors in tubes and brushes in various shapes

Working with watercolors

All watercolors are used on watercolor papers. You can blend colors and depending on how much water you put in, you get very different results. Children with ASD often try to paint in their own way, ignoring the directions, and end up getting upset, as they do not get the result they hoped for with this media. Once they understand that it is important for them to pay attention and accept help as needed, they do learn to accept new ways gradually.

Ted loved creating dots and circles on his paintings. He created small bubbles and tried to paint the background around the bubbles. This was very time consuming and required good fine motor skills as well as delicate balance of paint with water. It is much easier to paint the background first, wait to dry and make bubbles with thick paint. He insisted on using a thick paint brush to paint around the circle. The circles got smaller each time he painted and smeared the circles. He tried to fix the circle by painting over with the thick paint brush. By this time he was extremely upset and needed sensory input to calm down.

In order for him to accept a new way to paint or use various sizes of paint brushes to paint around the bubbles, we needed some time for him to trust me and understand that he could work better without getting frustrated if he accepted my help. Reassurance and visual demonstration helped him most. Previously, I never thought painting with watercolor was complicated, but we take for granted the many skills and decisions it takes to paint pictures.

Working with BioColor paints

Figure 17: Biocolor paint, Liquid water color and tempera

These are child safe paints created by Discount School Supply. It is similar to acrylic paint and you can paint over when it is dry. You can pour it over a plastic sheet and when it is dry, you can peel it off and you have window stickers.

When blended with Bio Putty Solution, you get silly putty.

MODELING

Natural clay—Natural clay is clay dug up from the earth and processed to use for pottery. Many people report that the sensory experience with the clay helps them to calm down.

The finished art works need to be fired in the kiln. Make sure to have tools to increase creativity (Figure 18).

Air dry clay—This paper based clay hardens in a few days and can be painted. Some inexpensive ones from Crayola tend to deteriorate over time.

Model Magic—I found this air dry clay is suitable for the people with sensory sensitivity. It is sticky but does not stick to your hands. When it is dried, you can apply vanish. It comes in various colors but you can paint both before and after it hardens.

Homemade play dough— A gluten-free diet is not proven to be effective for people with ASD but many parents have found it is helpful to reduce difficult behavior. As an art media, this rice based dough is very soft and gentle to the touch. See the recipe on the last page of this chapter.

Modeling Tools

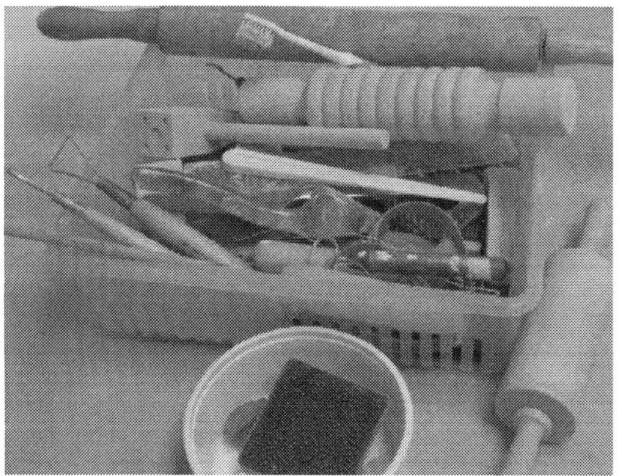

Figure 18: Modeling tools

MATERIALS TO INCREASE IMAGINATION AND IDEAS

- Stencils
- Templates
- Precut shapes
- Geometric shapes
- Visual materials related to their interests. Use books and an iPad with Google images.

GLUES

You may wonder why I specifically write about glue. Over 30 years of working with children, I have had a lot of troubles working with glue. Elmer's white glue used to have caps that were always clogged. Glue sticks are not cheap and many children like to roll out the glue stick too long and it breaks and smears all over the place. I began putting glue into small containers for applying it with a brush. The problem then is where to put the paint brush with sticky glue. In the end, I found keeping runny glue in a soft squeeze bottle (Figure20) and spreading glue with a paint brush seems to work best.

Children with ASD and sensory issues may like the stickiness of the glue or they may not. If the child is overly sensitive to stickiness and engaged in an activity requiring glue, having sticky glue on his hands may become a huge problem! Instead of entirely avoiding projects needing glue, I help them to gradually get used to the glue and make sure to have a wet towel to wipe their hands. Other children may enjoy the stickiness of the glue and the art project may become entirely different.

Here are some alternative adhesives (Figure 19)

- Clear glue in squeeze bottle
- Glue Dots Adhesives
- Double sided tapes
- Contact papers(no image in Figure 19)
- Spray glue

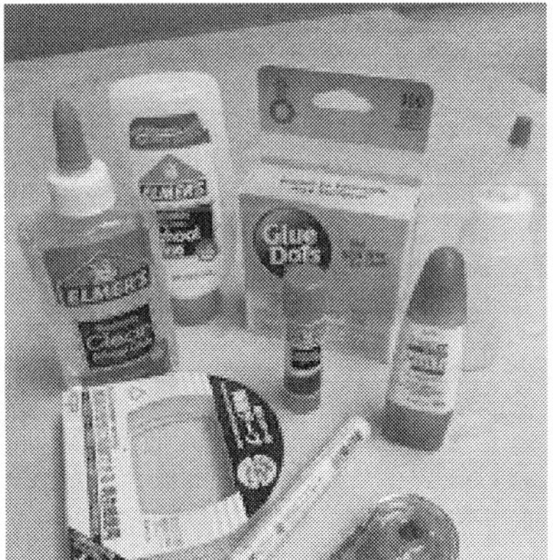

- Figure 19: glues

OTHER MEDIA

- Tapes
- Mixed textured papers, fabric and shapes
- Stapled papers to make books
- Puzzle and mosaic designs
- Glue paint (Figure 20)

For glue paint, I mix liquid water colors with clear glue into squeeze bottles. Some children like the sensory experience of squeezing. Despite the stickiness of the contents of the bottle, you can paint without dealing with it.

Figure 20: Glue paint

Other crafts as therapy

KNITTING

I think knitting may be therapeutic for people with ASD. As you move the right and left needles, you use both right and left brain bilaterally. This is similar to the Bio Lateral tools that therapists use in EMDR therapy to lower anxiety and help the right and left brain work together. Many people with ASD struggle to coordinate these right and left movements so it may be challenging, but the patterns in the knitting would likely attract people with spatial visual skills. Herbert Benson, in the book *The Relaxation Response*, says that the repetitive action of needlework can induce a relaxed state like that associated with meditation and yoga.

ORIGAMI

Origami is an excellent media for the people with high spatial / visual skills. Because of their interest in the activity, we can get their full attention to observe and imitate.

Art Themes and Activities

The book *Drawing Autism* (2011) shows the various themes that people with ASD like to create. In previous chapters I discussed specific themes. Some of their repetitive images are visually interesting, but just as Jessy Park's mother helped Jessy to paint houses instead of electric panels, we would like to use art activities to help people with ASD to connect and thrive in the Typically Developing (TD) world. For this reason they need help to broaden their area of interest.

The introduction to a new activity should be slow and gradual. The trust and visual directions are two important factors for their changes.

Social stories and other book making

Take several sheets of copy paper and staple them together.

Some children like to have their art works to be covered and enjoy looking at their art works like a book. With more verbal children, you may make social stories using their original drawings instead of board maker images. The board maker is computer software to create picture communication symbols.

Seasonal Activities

These might be more suitable to do in classrooms, but occasionally I include a seasonal art project to broaden interests. Many seasonal activities below contain sensory stimulation and possibilities for storytelling. Not all the **activities are suitable for every person with ASD.**

January- Snow men	
 Figure 21: January- Snow Scene, Snow Men	Use paint and paper collage on colored paper

February-Valentine's Day	
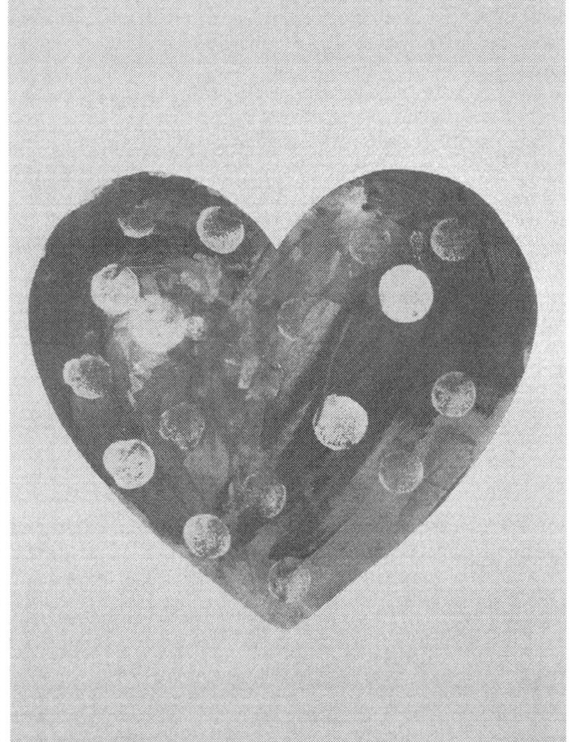 Figure 22: February-Valentine's day card	Using paint and glued paper of various textures and sizes, create a heart shaped greeting card

<table>
<tr><td colspan="2">March- St. Patrick's Day</td></tr>
<tr><td>
Figure 23: March
St. Patrick's day project</td><td>Cut out heart shapes and glue various colors of tissue papers and fabric. For St. Patrick's Day, combine three hearts to make clover.</td></tr>
</table>

<table>
<tr><td colspan="2">April- Easter</td></tr>
<tr><td>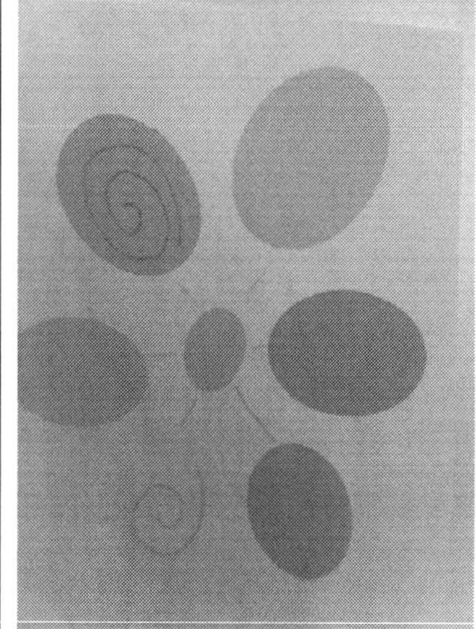
Figure 24: April
Easter collage project</td><td>Cut out egg shapes and glue various colors of tissue papers and fabric.</td></tr>
</table>

May- Spring	
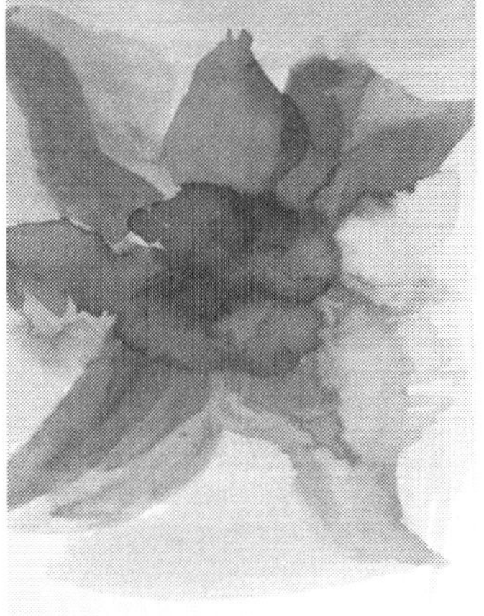 Figure 25: May Spring flower project	Spring flowers water colors– play with water and liquid water colors

September- Starting School	
 Figure 26: September Fall wreath project	Lightly sponge orange, red, and/or yellow paint on red and green construction paper and when those are dry, trace shapes of leaves. Glue around a paper plate to create a class wreath

<table>
<tr><td colspan="2">October- Halloween</td></tr>
<tr><td>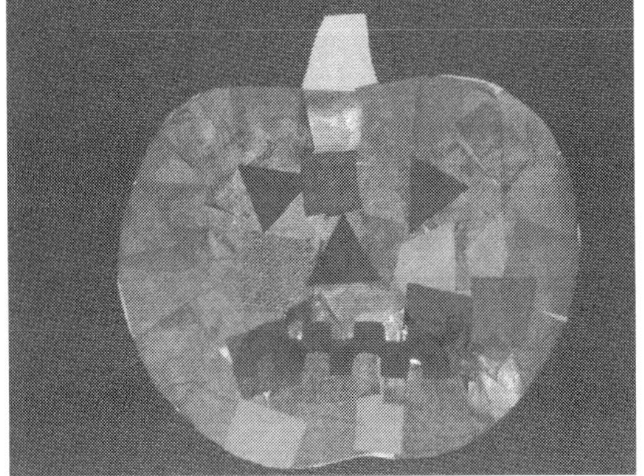
Figure 27: October
Feeling Jack-o-Lantern</td><td>Glue tissue paper and construction paper to create a jack-o-lantern that expresses your feeling</td></tr>
</table>

<table>
<tr><td colspan="2">November- Thanksgiving</td></tr>
<tr><td>
Figure 28: November
Thanksgiving collage</td><td>Glue paper plates and photos of food</td></tr>
</table>

December- Christmas	
 Figure 29: December Christmas story collage	Using precut shapes, create a holiday scene and stories.

GLUTEN-FREE PLAY DOUGH RECIPE

Based on the recipe on NFCA website. Gluten-free play dough is not only safe for the people on a gluten-free diet, but also its texture is softer and more sensory friendly for people with ASD.

Ingredients:

- 1/2 cup rice flour
- 1/2 cup cornstarch
- 1/2 cup salt
- 2 teaspoons cream of tartar
- 1 tablespoon olive oil or other vegetable oil

Tools:

- Medium size pot
- Cooking spoon
- Measuring cup, and teaspoon and tablespoon
- Heating source
- 1 cup warm water

Food coloring or liquid water color (optional)

☆You can find both rice flour and cream of tartar in the bulk section of your local grocery store. Cream of tartar in the regular spice section is way too expensive. I found cornstarch is cheaper when you buy the packaged one.

Directions:

1. Combine first four dry ingredients into a pot and mix gently together with a cooking spoon.

2. Add oil and warm water and continue mixing all ingredients.

3. Heat the pot over low heat, stirring mixture constantly until a ball of dough forms.

4. Remove the teaspoon dough from heat and let cool.

5. Once the dough is cool enough, knead the dough to the desired consistency. You may add water or corn starch to make the dough softer or dryer. You may knead with food coloring or liquid water color.

☆If you like stickier dough, increase the amount of rice flour. It turns whiter as you increase the rice flour. Do not overheat the dough. Once it starts sticking together, sometimes the heat of the pot is enough to form the dough. Oil prevents the dough from sticking to your hands but sometimes you may find it too greasy. Change the amount depending on you/your child's sensory needs.

☆ The dough keeps a long time since it contains a lot of salt. You may keep it in your refrigerator to be on the safe side. I find the tactile experience of warm dough after cooking and cold dough after keeping it in the refrigerator can be a nice sensory exercise.

☆ I like blending three primary colors; red, yellow and blue with the dough. Many children with ASD like colors and color theory. Help them to learn how to make different colors out of three primary colors of play dough.

References

American Art Therapy Association. (2014). Art therapy & Autism Spectrum Disorder: Integrating creative interventions. Retrieved from: http://www.arttherapy.org/AutismToolkit/autismtoolkit.pdf

American Psychiatric Association. (2013). *Diagnostic and statistical manual of mental disorders* (5th Ed.). Washington, DC and London, UK: American Psychiatric Publishing.

Baron-Cohen, S. (1987). Autism and symbolic play. *British Journal of Developmental Psychology*, 5(2), 139-148.

Baron-Cohen, S. (1995). *Mindblindness: An essay on autism and theory of mind*. Cambridge, MA. MIT Press.

Baron-Cohen, S. (2001). Theory of mind in normal development and autism. *Prisme*, 174-183.

Baron-Cohen, S. (2002). The extreme male brain theory of autism. *Trends in Cognitive Sciences, 6(6)*, 248-254.

Baron-Cohen, S., Scott, F. J., Allison, C., Williams, J., Bolton, P., Matthews, F. E., & Brayne, C. (2009). Prevalence of autism-spectrum conditions: UK school-based population study. *The British Journal of Psychiatry, 194,* 500-509.

Belkofer, C. (2008). Conducting art therapy research using quantitative EEG measure. *Art Therapy: Journal of the American Art Therapy Association, 28(4),* 56-63.

Benson, H. (2000). *The Relaxation Response*. New York, NY: Harper Collins Publishers.

Berube, C. T. (2007). Autism and the artistic imagination: The link between visual thinking and intelligence. *TEACHING Exceptional Children Plus*, 3(5).

Brooke, S. L. (Ed.). (2009).*The use of the creative therapies with autism spectrum disorders.* Springfield, IL: Charles C. Thomas Publisher.

Drake, J.E., et al. (2010). Autistic local processing bias also found in children gifted in realistic drawing. *Journal of Autism and Developmental Disorders*, 40, 762-773.

Drake, J.E. and A. Hodge. (2014). Drawing vs. writing: The role of preference in regulating short-term affect. *Art Therapy: Journal of the American Art Therapy Association*.

Grandin, T. (2006). *Thinking in pictures, expanded edition: My life with autism*. New York, NY : Vintage Books.

Grandin, T. and Panek, R. (2013). *The autistic brain: Thinking across the spectrum*. New York, NY: Houghton Mifflin Harcourt.

Benson, H. (2000). *The relaxation response*. New York, NY: Harper Collins Publishers.

Kunda, M and Goel, A. K. (2010). Thinking in pictures as a cognitive account of autism. *Journal of Autism and Developmental Disorders, 41,* 1157-1177. Doi: 10.1007/s10803-010-1137-1

Koshino, H et al. (2005). Functional connectivity in an fMRI working memory task in high functioning autism.

Neuroimage, 24, 810-821. Retrieved from: http://www.elsevier.com/locate/ynimg

Kozhevnikov, M., Kosslyn, S., & Shephard, J. (2005). Spatial versus object visualizers: A new characterization of visual cognitive style. *Memory & Cognition, 33*(4), 710-726.

Kozhevnikov, M., Kozhevnikov, M., Yu, C. J., & Blazhenkova, O. (2013). Creativity, visualization abilities, and visual cognitive style. *British Journal of Educational Psychology, 83(*2), 196-209.

Kramer, E. (1983). An art therapy evaluation session for children. *American Journal of Art Therapy 23(*1), Oct 1983, 3-12.

Kubler-Ross, E. (1969). *On Death and Dying*. New York, NY: Scribner, Simon&Schuster, Inc.

Lacour, K. (2013). The value of art therapy for those on the autism spectrum. Retrieved from http://the-art-of-autism.com

Lindgren, S. and Doobay, A. (2011) Evidence Based Interventions for Autism Spectrum Disorders. University of Iowa Hospitals and Clinics.

Lowenfeld, V. (1987). *Creative and mental growth*. New York, NY: Macmillan Publishing Company.

Martin, N. (2008). Assessing portrait drawings created by children and adolescents with Autism Spectrum Disorder. *Art Therapy: Journal of the American Art Therapy Association, 25*(1), 15-23.

Martin, N. (2009). Art therapy and autism: Overview and recommendation. *Art Therapy: Journal of the American Art Therapy Association, 26*(4), 187-190.

Martin, N. (2009). *Art as an early intervention tool for children with autism*. London, UK and Philadelphia, PA: Jessica Kingsley Publishers.

Miller, E. (2008). *The girl who spoke with pictures: Autism through art.* London and Philadelphia, PA: Jessica Kingsley Publishers.

Mullin, J. (2009). *Drawing autism*. New York, NY. Akashic Books.

Nicols, S. (2009). *Girls growing up on the autism spectrum*. London, UK and Philadelphia PA: Jessica Kingsley Publishers.

Park, C. C. (2001). *Exiting nirvana: A daughter's life with autism*. New York, NY. Hachette Book Group.

Sacks, O. (1987). *The man who mistook his wife for a hat*. New York, NY. Touchstone.

Sacks, O. (1995). *An anthropologist on Mars*. New York, NY. Vintage Books.

Sacks, O. (1996). *Rage of order*. Retrieved from https://www.youtube.com/

Selfe, L. (2011). *Nadia revisited: A longitudinal study of an autistic savant*. New York, NY. Psychology Press.

Scott, F. (2013). The development of imagination in children with autism. In Taylor, M. Editor, *The Oxford Handbook of the Development of Imagination* (499). New York, NY. Oxford University Press.

Silberman, S. (2015). *Neurotribes: The legacy of autism and the future of neurodiversity*. New York, NY. Penguin Random House.

Soulieres, I. (2009). Enhanced visual processing contributes to matrix reasoning in autism. *Human Brain Mapping, 30,* 4082-4107. Retrieved from: http://www.interscience.wiley.com

Stevenson, J et al. (2013). Abstract spatial reasoning as an autistic strength. *PLOS ONE 8(*3). Retrieved from http://www.plosone.org

Ulman, P. (2014). Art Therapy and Children with Autism: Gaining Access to Their World Through Creativity. Retrieved from http://www.arttherapy.org/autismtoolkit/ullmann.pdf

Vital, P.M., Ronald A., Wallace GL., Happe, F. (2009). Relationship between special abilities and autistic-like traits in a large population-based sample of 8-year-olds. *Journal of Child Psychology and Psychiatry, 50 (9),* 1093-1101.

Wong, C., Odom, S.L., Hume, K, Cox, A. W, Fetting, A., Kucharczyk, S., Brock, M. E., Plavnick, J. B., Fleury, V. P. and Schultz, T. R. (2014). Evidence-based practices for children, youth, and young adults with Autism Spectrum Disorder. Chapel Hill: The University of North Carolina, Frank Porter Graham Child Development Institute, Autism Evidence-Based Practice Review Group. Retrieved from http://autismpdc.fpg.unc.edu/sites/autismpdc.fpg.unc.edu/files/2014-EBP-Report.pdf

Zaidel, D. W. (2005) *Neuropsychology of art: Neurological, cognitive and evolutionary perspectives.* New York, NY: Psychology Press.

Web Sites

American Art Therapy Association. http://www.arttherapy.org/AutismToolkit/autismtoolkit.pf

The Art of Autism http://the-art-of-autism.com/

Autism Speaks. https://www.autismspeaks.org/

Center for Disease Control and Prevention(CDC). http://www.cdc.gov/ncbddd/autism/data.html

Center for Speech and Language Disorder. http://www.csld.org/

Interactive Autism Network. https://iancommunity.org/

National Autistic Society. http://www.autism.org.uk/

Sensory Processing Disorder Foundation. http://www.spdfoundation.net/about-sensory-processing-disorder/

About the author

Mia (Mineko) is a Registered Art Therapist and Licensed Mental Health Counselor in private practice in Bellevue and Seattle, Washington.

She has B.A in fine art painting from Musashino Art University in Tokyo and M.A. in Art Therapy from New York University.

Before moving to Seattle in 1994, Mia taught art in Honduras and worked with children with special needs in the Japanese Special Education School in Nara, Japan.

Before starting her private practice, Mia worked with children and their families in a community mental health agency, various school districts, and at Childhaven, a non-profit agency serving abused and at risk young children.

She lives in Seattle, Washington with her husband, her son, who created the cover of this book, and two border collies. She is training the younger dog to work as a therapy dog.

She likes creating her art with clay and mosaic as well as enameling on metal.

Please visit her website, www.studiomene.com for more information

Made in the USA
San Bernardino, CA
07 September 2016